Tunisia

D1377865

This book, *Tunisia: Stability and reform in the modern Maghreb*, gives a concise yet comprehensive overview of Tunisia's political and economic development from the mid-nineteenth century to the present. Written specifically for a non-specialist audience, the book examines the factors that make Tunisia one of the Arab world's most stable and prosperous countries and one of its hardiest authoritarian orders. The author explores these themes in a way that sheds light on the political dynamics of the broader Arabic-speaking, Muslim world.

Christopher Alexander draws on extensive primary and secondary research and on comparison with other countries in the region to provide the most up-to-date introduction to Tunisia's post-independence politics. Challenging the notion that Tunisia's stability is rooted in a unique political culture, he argues that Tunisia's stability reflects the pragmatic interests of a wide range of actors and the skillful maneuvering of the country's two presidents.

Concisely written, chapters cover topics such as:

- state formation
- domestic politics
- economic development
- foreign relations
- colonialism

An essential inclusion on courses on Middle Eastern politics, African politics, and political science in general, this accessible introduction to Tunisia will also be of interest to anyone wishing to learn more about this significant region.

Christopher Alexander is the John and Ruth McGee Director of the Dean Rusk International Studies Program at Davidson College, North Carolina, USA. He also teaches courses in International Relations and Middle East Politics in Davidson's Department of Political Science.

The Contemporary Middle East
Edited by Professor Anoushiravan Ehteshami
Institute for Middle Eastern and Islamic Studies, University of Durham

For well over a century now the Middle Eastern and North African countries have formed a central plank of the international system. *The Contemporary Middle East* series provides the first systematic attempt at studying the key actors of this dynamic, complex, and strategically important region. Using an innovative common format—which in each case study provides an easily-digestible analysis of the origins of the state, its contemporary politics, economics and international relations—prominent Middle East experts have been brought together to write definitive studies of the MENA region's key countries.

Books in the series:

Tunisia

Stability and reform in the modern Maghreb

Christopher Alexander

Routledge
Taylor & Francis Group

LONDON AND NEW YORK

First published 2010
by Routledge
2 Park Square, Milton Park, Abingdon, Oxon OX14 4RN

Simultaneously published in the USA and Canada
by Routledge
270 Madison Avenue, New York, NY 10016

*Routledge is an imprint of the Taylor & Francis Group,
an informa business*

Typeset in Sabon by RefineCatch Ltd, Bungay, Suffolk
Printed and bound in Great Britain by
TJ International Ltd, Padstow, Cornwall

British Library Cataloguing in Publication Data
A catalogue record for this book is available from the British Library

Library of Congress Cataloging in Publication Data
Alexander, Christopher
  Tunisia : stability and reform in the modern Maghreb / Christopher
  Alexander.
    p. cm.—(The contemporary Middle East ; 9)
  Includes bibliographical references and index.
  1. Political stability—Tunisia. 2. Authoritarianism—Tunisia.
  3. Tunisia—Politics and government—1987– I. Title.
  JQ3330.A44 2010
  320.9611—dc22   2009035612

ISBN10: 0–415–27421–4 (hbk)
ISBN10: 0–415–48330–1 (pbk)
ISBN10: 0–203–88412–4 (ebk)

ISBN13: 978–0–415–27421–0 (hbk)
ISBN13: 978–0–415–48330–8 (pbk)
ISBN13: 978–0–203–88412–6 (ebk)

Contents

Acknowledgements

This book spent far too long on the computer screen. First thanks must go to the good people at Taylor & Francis and its Middle East and Asian Studies series. They showed me the patience of Job. At Davidson College's Dean Rusk International Studies Program, Cristy Atkinson, Will Hummel, and Larissa Hohe made it possible for me to disappear for extended stretches of writing time. Athan Makansi provided excellent research assistance. Alex Gregor and Mark Iafrate in Davidson's Instructional Technology and Media staff provided wonderful help preparing the map of Tunisia. Clark Ross, Davidson's Dean of the Faculty, provided steady encouragement, as did Mr John "Doodle" Wally. As much as I like him, I dreaded seeing Doodle on campus because I knew that the first words out of his mouth would be, "Have you finished your book yet"? His good-natured prodding laid a helpful crop to my flanks. Carol, Nell, and Malcolm provided the kind of daily love and support that only family can provide. As an author herself, Carol knows how jealous book manuscripts inevitably become. Her encouragement and patience made this possible.

Abbreviations

ASQ	*Association pour la Sauvegarde de Quran* (Association for the Preservation of the Qur'an)
CNLT	*Comité National pour les Libertés en Tunisie* (National Committee for Liberties in Tunisia)
FDTL	*Forum Démocratique pour les Libertés et le Travail* (Democratic Forum for Liberties and Labor)
GEAST	*Groupe d'études et d'action socialiste tunisien* (Group for Tunisian Socialist Study and Action)
GSPC	*Groupe Salafiste pour la Prédication et le Combat* (Salafist Group for Preaching and Combat)
IMF	International Monetary Fund
ISI	import-substituting industrialization
LTDH	*Ligue Tunisienne des Droits de l'Homme* (Tunisian Human Rights League)
MDS	*Mouvement des Démocrates Socialistes* (Movement of Social Democrats)
MTI	*Mouvement de la Tendance Islamique* (Islamic Tendency Movement)
MUP	*Mouvement de l'Unité Populaire* (Popular Unity Movement)
OPEC	Organization of Petroleum Exporting Countries
PCT	*Parti Communiste Tunisien* (Tunisian Communist Party)
PLO	Palestine Liberation Organization
POCT	*Parti Ouvrier Communiste Tunisien* (Tunisian Communist Worker Party)
PSD	*Parti Socialist Destourien* (Destourian Socialist Party)
PSL	*Parti Social-Libéral* (Social-Liberal Party)
PUP	*Parti de l'Unité Populaire* (Popular Unity Party)
PVP	*Parti des Verts pour le Progrés* (Green Party for Progress)
RCD	*Rassemblement Constitutionnel Démocratique* (Democratic Constitutional Rally)
RSP	Progressive Socialist Rally
TIFA	Trade and Investment Framework Agreement
UDU	*Union Démocratique Unionist* (Democratic Unionist Union)

UGET	*Union Générale des Étudiants de Tunisie* (General Union of Tunisian Students)
UGTT	*Union Générale, Tunisienne de Travail* (General Tunisian Labor Union)
UMA	*Union du Maghreb Arab* (Arab Maghreb Union)
USAID	United States Agency for International Development
UTT	*Union Tunisienne de Travail* (Tunisian Labor Union)

Chronology

1100 BC	Early Phoenician settlements
circa 800	Carthage established
263–146	Punic Wars
429–535 AD	Vandal invasion and rule
647	Arab armies defeat Byzantines at Sbeitla
670	Arab army under Oqba Ibn Nafi establishes Kairouan as the base for their expansion across the Maghreb
800–900	Aghlabid rule
909–70	Fatimid rule
1236–1534	Hafsid rule; Tunis becomes capital
1300–1570s	Spain and Turkey struggle for control of North Africa
1574	Tunisia becomes part of the Ottoman Empire
1705	Husaynid dynasty established
1860	Tunisia's first constitution
1881	French occupation and declaration of Protectorate
1907	Young Tunisians established
1911–12	First nationalist unrest erupts in Tunis
1920	Destour Party established
1934	Neo-Destour Party established
1956	Tunisia proclaims independence on March 20
1961	Beginning of centralized, planned economic development strategy; armed conflict with France over Bizerte
1964	Tunisia nationalizes French holdings; Neo-Destour changes its name to the *Parti Socialist Destourien*
1969–70	End of the collectivization program and the beginning of *infitah*
1970–72	Association for the Safeguard of the Qur'an established
1972–74	New investment laws strengthen incentives for private investment
1974	National Assembly declares Bourguiba president for life; brief union with Libya in the Arab Islamic Republic
1975	Tunisian Human Rights League established

1978	UGTT launches first general strike in post-independence history on January 26
1980	Tunisian commandos, with Libyan support, attack southern town of Gafsa of January 26
1984	Riots break out across the country after the government cuts subsidies for basic consumer goods
1985	Israeli forces bomb PLO headquarters in a Tunis suburb
1986	Tunisia adopts structural adjustment plans supported by the IMF and the World Bank
1987	Zine al-Abidine Ben Ali deposes Habib Bourguiba on November 7
1988	Government, opposition parties, and civil society organizations sign National Pact; Israeli commandos assassinate PLO military chief in Tunis
1989	Arab Maghreb Union established; April elections reveal Ennahdha as strongest opposition party
1990–92	Government launches crackdown on Ennahdha
1994	Limited proportionality introduced into legislative elections
1995	Tunisia becomes first Maghreb country to sign an association agreement with the EU
1998	National Committee for Liberties in Tunisia established
1999	First multi-candidate presidential election
2002	Islamist militants bomb synagogue on the island of Djerba; constitutional reform lifts term limits on the presidency and creates Chamber of Advisors; Tunisia and the US sign Trade and Investment Framework Agreement
2005	End of multi-fiber protections for Tunisian textiles
2008	Beginning of industrial free trade zone between Tunisia and EU

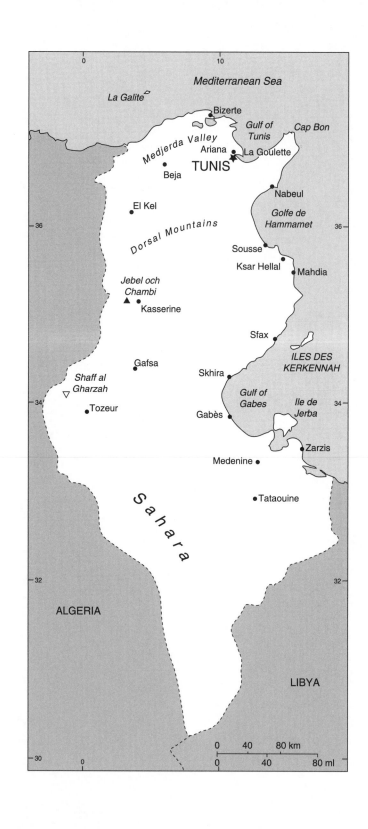

Introduction

Writing at the close of the nineteenth century, the British author Herbert Vivian opined that "[t]he authorities on Tunisia are not worth enumerating. Those in English belong to a former generation; those in French are prejudiced and stupid" (1899: vii).

This was harsh language in Vivian's day; it is untrue and unfair in ours. Over the past fifty years, Tunisia has been the subject of considerable and very fine work in both English and French. Nevertheless, few countries in the Arab world remain less familiar to English speakers than Tunisia. Several factors account for this lack of attention. Tunisia is a small country. Its population numbers just more than 10 million across an area slightly smaller than the state of Florida or the United Kingdom without Scotland. It does not possess large quantities of oil, natural gas, or any other strategic resources. Politically, Tunisia has remained an inconspicuous island of calm in troubled seas. It was never caught up in the tumultuous wave of military coups and ideological conflicts that swept across much of the region in the 1950s and 1960s. It has never been more than a peripheral player in the Arab-Israeli conflict. In short, Tunisia has remained far removed from core American and British interests in the Arabic-speaking world.

Culturally, too, Tunisia seemed different from most of the Arab world. Although Arabic-speaking Sunni Muslims make up 98 percent of the population, Tunisia's post-independence elite and the culture of its rapidly growing cities reflect Europe's strong influence. As one former Minister of Culture put it to a visiting journalist not long ago, "Our reference groups are the French and the Italians, not the Algerians and Libyans" (Kaplan 2001). For visitors accustomed to Egypt, Jordan, Syria, Iraq, or the countries of the Arabian Peninsula, Tunisia often feels more "Mediterranean" than "Middle Eastern". Sitting at the crossroads of Africa, the Middle East, and Europe, Tunisia and its Maghreb neighbors developed rich cultures and complex politics.[1] But this location also meant that the region slipped between the geographical categories that shaped Anglo-American research for much of the twentieth century. Though linked to France, Spain, and Italy by proximity and colonial history, the Maghreb clearly was not part of Europe. But it also was not "African" in the way that most Western

Europeans and North Americans conceived of the continent. Its culture and its political and economic development more closely resembled other Arab countries, but it also differed from those countries in important ways. This ambiguity, combined with the absence of strong Anglo-American strategic interests and France's unique history in the region, made Maghrebi scholarship a predominantly French affair.

There are exceptions to this record of Anglo-American neglect. If one lays the books and articles written in English about Tunisia's political and economic development along a timeline, most of them fall into two periods. Both correspond to periods when scholars and policymakers held up Tunisia as a model for others to emulate. The first period occurred in the 1960s, when Tunisia exemplified the orderly, progressive modernization that analysts hoped would unfold across the developing world in the decades following the Second World War. Under President Habib Bourguiba, Tunisia's single-party system was authoritarian enough to provide stability while remaining open to new constituencies and responsive to new concerns. The government pursued a pro-Western policy abroad and a pragmatic development strategy that raised living standards at home.

Interest in Tunisia dropped in the 1970s and early 1980s. Events elsewhere in the region bore some responsibility for the decline. The rise of the PLO and the intensifying conflict between Palestinians and Israelis, the 1973 Arab-Israeli war, the OPEC oil embargo, civil war in Lebanon, the Camp David peace process, revolution in Iran, the initial stirrings of Islamist political movements in several countries—all of these developments drew scholarly attention away from North Africa.

But domestic developments also played an important role in reducing interest in Tunisia. By the early 1970s, it was clear that Tunisia's political and economic development path would not be as straight and smooth as many analysts had expected. Internal political challenges arose that the ruling party could not contain without becoming more visibly authoritarian. The economy struggled to generate growth for a young and growing population. Widespread discontent over the government's authoritarianism and mounting economic hardship turned the decade from 1975–85 into one of the most difficult in Tunisia's modern history. Tunisia no longer stood as a model for other countries to follow.

Despite these challenges, Tunisia's unrest never posed a serious threat to the government's survival. As contentious as Tunisia became, Bourguiba's rule never seemed in serious jeopardy until the final months before his fall in November 1987. Thus, if Tunisia no longer offered a model of stable development, neither did it provide a case of dramatic political change that could generate useful lessons for scholars or policymakers. It was just another messy developing country. In the absence of clear strategic or social scientific importance, Tunisia drifted off most British and American scholars' research agendas.

It returned in the late 1980s, when a new set of economic and political challenges made Tunisia look a good deal more like its Middle Eastern and North African neighbors. Like other countries in the region, Tunisia confronted the pressing need for structural economic reform and an Islamist movement that eclipsed traditional opposition organizations. When Zine al-Abidine Ben Ali seized power from Bourguiba in a bloodless coup in November 1987, he promised a broad range of substantial political and economic reforms. Many observers believed that Tunisia would demonstrate how liberal economic and political reform could work together in the Arab world. Many of the social, political, and economic characteristics that contributed to Tunisia's peaceful modernization in the 1950s and 1960s got held up again as strong aids to democratization in the late 1980s. Once again, Tunisia would be a model. It would yield insights into how political and economic liberalization could create robust growth and stable democracies in a region dominated by stagnation and authoritarianism. This prospect drew a new generation of scholars to Tunisia, including this author. At least among the political scientists, many of us had received training that emphasized the substance and the tools of economics more than culture. We scurried about, mostly in Tunis, talking with government officials, business owners and their associations, workers and their unions, leaders of secular and Islamist opposition parties, all in an effort to understand how political actors define their interests and make choices during periods of critical change.

We discovered a country whose experience defied easy generalizations about a comfortable partnership between economic and political reform. On the economic front, the government's policies generated one of the most impressive records in the Middle East and North Africa. By the mid-1990s, the International Monetary Fund, the World Bank, and most Western governments hailed Tunisia as one of the best exemplars of structural economic reform. In this respect, Tunisia had again become a model.

In its politics, however, Tunisia remained a very authoritarian place. In fact, some argue that it has been more authoritarian in the first decade of the twenty-first century than it was thirty years ago. There was a healthy rowdiness to Tunisian politics in the 1970s and the early 1980s. Unions struck; respected political leaders left the ruling party and established opposition parties; civil society organizations struggled for greater independence; students demonstrated for fundamental political and economic change. Even if Tunisia was an authoritarian place, substantive political debate did take place. By the mid-1990s, however, the rowdiness was gone. The government deftly hijacked the opposition's democratic rhetoric while it waged open war against anyone who dared to criticize the president and the ruling party.

This authoritarianism chilled much of the scholarly interest in Tunisian politics. At the end of the day, all political outcomes seemed to share the same explanation—they all reflected what the president wanted. No matter how hard one dug to find some more complex and subterranean politics, the tunnel always led to the presidential palace. If this simple explanation was accurate, then Tunisian politics had lapsed into another period of theoretical irrelevance. Tunisia's experience had little to say to scholars whose research in other countries focused on democratic change. If this explanation was not accurate, then it simply was too difficult to find and support others. Scholars with tight budgets and a desire to engage broader disciplinary questions could collect richer rewards for their labors in other countries. Thus, while an occasional newspaper article applauded the government's economic reforms or criticized its human rights abuses, new books and articles about Tunisian politics became scarcer after the mid-1990s.

With all of that as backdrop, why should anyone bother to write or read a book about Tunisia's modern economic and political development? At least two powerful reasons commend the effort. First, Tunisia and its Maghreb neighbors play an important, if not very public, role in contemporary conversations about European and North American security. Indeed, the Maghreb may be more important to US and European security interests now than ever before. Algeria's civil war, bombings in Morocco and Tunisia, and the role that activists with North African roots have played in Islamist activities in Europe, Iraq, and Afghanistan make the region increasingly important in its own right and as a transition zone between Europe, Africa, and the Middle East.

Understanding Tunisia is also important because it sheds interesting light on political challenges facing the Middle East and North Africa. More than a decade after the end of the Cold War, the Middle East and North Africa stands as the last region in which authoritarian government is the thriving rule rather than the tottering exception. As noted above, this state of affairs is particularly noteworthy in Tunisia because the country is so richly endowed with factors that we often associate with democratic change: liberal economic policies, sustained economic growth, a long history of economic and cultural openness, a robust middle class, education and living standards that put Tunisia on par with some European countries, and some of the region's most progressive social legislation. Understanding why this combination of factors has not generated more democracy, or at least more pressure for it, has relevance beyond Tunisia.

Much of the answer to this question lies in the strategies that Tunisia's two presidents have used to maintain authoritarian rule. Each president came to power under different circumstances and each brought different attributes to the job. If Tunisia has been consistently authoritarian, the contours of authoritarian rule have changed over time.

Part of the answer also lies in the relationship between the two values mentioned in this book's subtitle: stability and reform. This is a complex relationship in the politics of any country; it is particularly intimate and complicated in Tunisia. Stability, by almost any definition, is one of the country's most notable characteristics. It is a quality that almost all Tunisians believe is vital, including those who have worked at various times for substantial change. Tunisians and friends of Tunisia sometimes advance a cultural explanation for this broad commitment to stability. They say that Tunisians are the most cosmopolitan and open people in the Maghreb. They possess a gentle sophistication that breeds a distaste for extremism and violence, and a strong preference for stability and pragmatism.

Cultural generalizations of this broad sort run out of explanatory power quickly. If Tunisians exhibit a particularly strong attachment to stability, it is because the country's size, slim resource endowment, and geographic location make stability a prerequisite to all else for a diverse range of actors and interests. No matter how greatly their other goals may differ, all of them require stability in order to achieve those goals. This shared commitment to stability gives a clear advantage to defenders of an authoritarian status quo because it limits what others will do in the interest of change. In tandem with two presidents' assertive but savvy authoritarianism, the result is a political system that has proven very resistant to dramatic change.

But the same concern for stability has also contributed to reform. Rulers have consistently recognized that reform can help them to maintain stability and enhance their power. By proposing reform themselves, they can control its pace and manage its content in ways that make them stronger. This, in turn, creates real dilemmas for the proponents of change. On the one hand, they realize what the rulers are doing. They understand that rulers use their control of the reform process to protect their prerogatives and to thwart additional challenges to them. On the other hand, the reforms often do create meaningful new opportunities. Pressing for more risks generating instability that could endanger a broad range of interests, alienate those interests from the democratic cause, and provoke an authoritarian backlash that takes back some or all of the concessions the government has made. The result, then, is an ongoing bargaining process between players who all value stability and reform, but who care about them for different ultimate reasons. The game changes over time as the players' interests and capabilities change.

The first chapter of this book roots Tunisia's modern political development in the colonial period and the struggle for independence. As Lisa Anderson (1986) argues, Tunisia has experienced a virtually uninterrupted process of state formation. Revolutionary change has never been part of the country's history. The French Protectorate made extensive use of pre-colonial institutions and practices in an effort to control Tunisia as cheaply as possible. At independence in 1956, the Neo-Destour—the nationalist party that led Tunisia to independence—stepped into and built upon the institutions vacated by the French. No change in the post-independence period, including the coup that brought Ben Ali to the presidency in 1987, has altered the basic structure of power and governance. While changes have taken place, none of them have threatened what one might describe as Tunisia's fundamental political order.

The first chapter also introduces another key theme in Tunisia's modern development: the combination of highly personalized power and a political party that tries to dominate all aspects of political and associational life. Contemporary scholars often resist analyzing the complex lives of whole states or nations in terms of single human beings. But the story of modern Tunisia is inseparable from the story of Habib Bourguiba, the man who led Tunisia's nationalist struggle and who served as president until 1987. As leader of the Neo-Destour party, Bourguiba built one of the most successful mass movements in the developing world. The party built a truly national structure that reached into every village, every social class, and every organization. Bourguiba and his allies argued that national unity was the prerequisite to independence. They cajoled and coerced divergent interests to lay aside their differences for the sake of building a single organization that would lead Tunisia to independence. But not everyone in the nationalist movement supported Bourguiba's strategy of negotiating independence in stages, or his secularism, or his general pro-Western orientation. Bourguiba's battle against internal opposition, and his feeling that he alone was destined to lead the country, produced a very personalized and authoritarian leadership style that left no room for the notion of loyal opposition.

Thus, Tunisia entered independence with a very strong ruling party and a very strong president who would not let anyone or any organization—including the party—limit his freedom of movement. Chapter 2 examines how these elements shaped post-independence politics. The fact that the Neo-Destour thoroughly monopolized the political and organizational landscape in Tunisia meant that the country benefitted from a strong, national structure that could take charge of the whole country at independence. However, that same monopoly, the same concept of national unity that served Tunisia well in its struggle for independence, deprived the country of any meaningful political or ideological counterweight to the Neo-Destour.

Under Bourguiba, Tunisia developed the appearance of a state corporatist system. In theory, this system brings together representatives of the government and representatives of official organizations that represent different components of society—students, workers, business owners, women, farmers. As the ultimate definer and defender to the broad national interest, the state establishes and maintains formal consultation and bargaining processes that allow these organizations to negotiate the policies that affect their members and that resolve conflicts between them in a consistent, orderly fashion. To use language that became popular in Tunisia in the 1970s, the state and these official organizations work together as "social partners" for the good of their members and of the nation as a whole.

Tunisia developed the trappings of such a system, but not its substance. The ruling party became indistinguishable from the state and it worked to dominate all forms of associational life. The party/state bureaucracy wanted unions and other corporatist organizations to implement its own policies, not to represent their members' interests in a more independent way. Moreover, there was no real bargaining process. Bourguiba established himself as the maker and breaker of careers in a highly personalized leadership style that converted policy management into people management.

This method protected Bourguiba's freedom to maneuver as he saw fit. But it also left the country without sufficient institutions for checking presidential power, for expressing and reconciling competing interests, or for transferring presidential power from one person to another. Too much of the country's business was conducted through Bourguiba's manipulation of a handful of key individuals. This highly personalized style, and Bourguiba's sense that no one else could replace him, limited his willingness to use reform to relieve mounting tensions in the 1970s and 1980s.

Tunisian politics has continued to be very authoritarian under Ben Ali. But Ben Ali's authoritarianism differs from Bourguiba's in important respects. Ben Ali's style has been very centralized, but much less personalized. While Bourguiba constructed a state corporatist façade over a highly personalized management style, Ben Ali has constructed a liberal democratic façade over a centralized and insulated technocracy. He successfully hijacked most of the secular opposition's themes with rhetoric that emphasized human rights, individual liberty, and political competition. He made it easier for new parties to form, to run in elections, and to win seats. He even has allowed other candidates to run for the presidency—something Bourguiba could not have fathomed. But Ben Ali's government has carefully crafted these reforms in ways that set very real limits on the amount of actual power that the opposition can win at the ballot box and the amount of criticism they can level through the media or human rights organizations. The result is a system that allows for greater competition within strict limits that the government defines and enforces vigorously. This less personalized authoritarianism has relied extensively on heavy-handed methods that have earned Ben Ali's government severe criticism from human rights groups. But the reforms have opened formal space for competition that did not exist under Bourguiba.

Chapter 3 shifts the focus to economics. Tunisia's post-independence economic development strategy has consistently reflected a form of state capitalism that pursues growth through private sector activity and integration into regional and global markets. However, political considerations have prompted the government to emphasize different components of its strategy at different times and to describe its policies in different terms. Thus, from independence through the early 1970s, the rhetoric of Tunisia's economic development strategy varied much more than the substance. Since the late 1980s, however, the gap between rhetoric and reality has been much narrower. Tunisia has been an unabashed proponent of liberal economic policies that emphasize growth through private foreign and domestic investment and through exports. But it has pursued these policies in ways that avoid some of their more socially disruptive—and politically dangerous—consequences. The chapter assesses the success of this strategy and discusses some of the challenges that lie ahead.

Chapter 4 turns to Tunisia's foreign relations. It focuses on the country's five most critical relationships or issue areas: France, the US, the European Union, the greater Middle East, and the Maghreb. As with the discussion of economics, the chapter emphasizes the stability that has marked Tunisia's core foreign policy interests and the degree to which domestic political considerations have shaped the government's defense of those interests. Tunisia's primary goal has been to maintain its independence and its freedom of action in an environment dominated by powerful neighbors and by various schemes that have threatened to unite Tunisia with one or more of them. Because the government has consistently preferred not to build a large military, deft diplomacy and strong relations with France and the US have been central to Tunisia's foreign policy. The government has also worked diligently to maintain French and European development assistance and to improve Tunisia's access to European markets. While all of the governments in the Maghreb have pledged allegiance to more extensive cooperation, particularly on economic issues, Tunisia has been the most serious proponent.

Devoting distinct chapters to politics, economics, and foreign relations makes it easier for readers to follow specific issue trajectories and to see how particular processes unfolded over time. However, the chapters make it abundantly clear that each of these issue areas strongly influences the others. It is impossible to understand Tunisia's economic or foreign policies at any given point in time without considering the domestic political situation. And one cannot understand domestic political developments without understanding the economic and regional environments. As in many developing countries, the distinctions between politics and economics in Tunisia, and between domestic and international issues, appear much more clearly on paper than in reality.

Thus, the concluding chapter steps above these boundaries to talk about Tunisia's future. It reflects on the complex relationship between stability and reform in Tunisia and on the reasons why this relationship has sustained authoritarian government rather than a transition to more meaningful democracy. It closes by discussing specific changes that need to take place in order to make democratic change more likely.

The point here is not to judge or to lecture. Only Tunisians can or should determine their country's course. But one of the most interesting things about Tunisian politics is the keenness of the trade-offs that Tunisians face. In light of the country's achievements over the past five decades, one can make a very credible argument in favor of the status quo. Tunisians enjoy a quality of life that is unrivalled in the region. Authoritarian government has contributed mightily to that. But one can also argue that what has worked well in the past may not do so over the long term. Tunisia may soon reach the limits of what its benevolent, pragmatic authoritarianism can provide.

Adapting to changing economic and political circumstances may require a new relationship between stability and reform—one that reduces the government's control over the reform process, but one that also involves a good deal more uncertainty. If that becomes the case, the concluding chapter identifies important hurdles to cross.

1 State-building and independence in Tunisia

Perched halfway down Tunisia's long eastern coast, the town of Ksar Hellal exudes more grit than grandeur. Like many other towns in the Sahel—the Arabic name for the belly of land that starts just south of Nabeul and stretches to the south of Sfax—it is an ancient and dusty place, cooled in the summer and chilled in the winter by the breeze off the Gulf of Monastir. The ruins of a Carthaginian town called Leptis Minor stand a very few kilometers away. Beyond its reputation as a tough textile town in a region known primarily for its olive trees, Ksar Hellal seems a rather unexceptional dot on the map. But in terms of Tunisia's modern political development, what happened here in early 1934 made history.

Just before sunset on January 3, two young men from Tunis arrived in town. Tahar Sfar and Habib Bourguiba shared much in common. Both hailed from the Sahel region. Both studied at Sadiki College, Tunisia's premier secondary school in Tunis, and both continued their educations in law and politics in Paris. Like many North Africans who studied or worked in Paris in the 1920s and 1930s, both young men became involved in the nationalist movement. They returned to Tunis to practice law and to build a stronger nationalist movement at home.

In early 1934, a bitter conflict wracked Tunisia's leading nationalist party, the Destour. Since the end of the First World War and the surge in nationalism that it generated, the Destour's leadership had relied on petitions, newspaper articles, and diplomatic delegations to encourage France to give Tunisians a larger role in their country's economic and political life. Those efforts had produced only superficial measures that did not reduce French domination in any meaningful way.

Led by Habib Bourguiba, younger members pressed for a more active strategy. They argued that France had broken its promise to be Tunisia's partner, to help Tunisians develop their economic and political systems in ways that would improve their lives. Instead, France had become a colonial overlord, controlling the government and the economy to serve French interests while most Tunisians remained poor and powerless. After years of fruitless petitions, articles, and delegations to Paris, the time had come to organize a broad-based movement that would steadily pressure France for reforms leading to full independence. Unable to convince conservative elements in the party to adopt a more confrontational strategy, Bourguiba and his allies concluded that they would have to break with the Destour's leadership and convince the rank and file to follow them.

That was the purpose of Bourguiba and Sfar's trip to Ksar Hellal in January, 1934. For three hours after an evening Ramadan meal, Bourguiba lectured local party members about the weakness of the Destour's leadership. He explained how a broad-based movement could unify all Tunisians behind a careful strategy that could withstand French repression, gain international support, and win independence in stages. By midnight, Bourguiba had won over his audience. He spent the next two months preaching the same message in other Sahel towns.[1] In March, he returned to Ksar Hellal and established the Neo-Destour—the organization that would lead Tunisia to independence and would become, in the words of one of the country's most respected observers, "possibly the most effective regime in the Afro-Asian world for leading its people toward a modern society" (Moore 1965: 8).

Landscape and Ottoman Institutions

The founding of the Neo-Destour marked the beginning of the end of French rule in Tunisia. But the party was itself the product of a prolonged process of economic, social, and political development. That process began quite slowly in the mid-nineteenth century and gained momentum in the early years of the twentieth.

On the eve of the French occupation in 1881, Tunisia looked much as it had for centuries. Compared to Algeria and Morocco, with their large Berber populations, Tunisian society remained quite homogeneous. Outside of small Jewish communities on the island of Djerba and in some neighborhoods of Tunis and a few larger towns, Arabic-speaking Sunni Muslims made up the overwhelming majority of the population. Differences in daily life and customs reflected differences between classes, between coastal and interior environments, and between settled and nomadic populations much more than differences in language, faith, or ethnicity (ibid.: 11–12). Towns and villages with long histories of sedentary agriculture dotted the Cap Bon peninsula and the Sahel. Then as now, fruit trees and irrigated vegetable gardens dominated the Cap Bon. Olive trees shaped culture and commerce in the Sahel. Wheat covered most of the north, particularly from the Medjerda Valley down through Beja, Jendouba, and Kef. South of the dorsal mountains and inland from Sousse and Sfax, small towns and farms gave way to a hot, dry pre-Saharan land of nomadic tribes in constant search of water and grazing lands to sustain flocks of sheep and goats (Anderson 1986: 36; Findlay 1984: 217–20).

Tunisia's incorporation into the Ottoman Empire in 1574 changed little of this landscape or its government. By that time, the government in Tunis already had a long history of virtual independence within a broader Muslim empire. Arab conquerors brought Islam to what was known then as *Ifriqiyya* in 670 AD. By the late eighth century, however, the Abbasid caliphs who ruled the growing Muslim empire from Baghdad faced serious challenges to their rule in far-flung North Africa and Spain. Local rulers had begun to operate with little regard for any direction from the capital.

From 800–1574, a succession of regional dynasties ruled *Ifriqiyya*: the Aghlabids, the Fatimids, the Almohads, and the Hafsids. These governments rarely wielded effective power over all of the territory that we now know as Tunisia. Under the Hafsids (1207–1574), the government in Tunis established more effective control over a larger area, expanded trade ties to Europe, and profited from piracy and the slave trade. More than any other pre-Ottoman dynasty, it is the Hafsids that modern Tunisians often regard as the founders of a Tunisian state.

But it was not a strong state—at least not strong enough to maintain its independence in the midst of the deepening conflict between Spain and Ottoman Turkey for control of the Mediterranean. That conflict prompted the Ottomans to seize Tunis in 1574. In the early years of their rule, the Ottomans divided authority between the *bey*, a civil administrator concerned primarily with tax collection; the *dey*, a military commander; and the *pasha*, the Ottoman sultan's representative. Given the intense regional conflict raging at the time, it is perhaps not surprising that the *deys*—the military authorities—wielded most of the power. Over time, however, the positions of *bey* and *pasha* combined, and the *bey* emerged as the preeminent authority.[2]

In 1705, the government in Istanbul appointed an Ottoman officer named Husayn ibn Ali to serve as bey of Tunis. In that position, Husayn enjoyed *de facto* sovereignty over Tunisia. As long as he kept the peace and paid taxes to Istanbul, he governed as he liked. He held all executive, legislative, and judicial authority. He exercised these powers with the assistance of a prime minister, a minister of the pen, and a central administration with sections dedicated to foreign, internal, and legal affairs (Ling 1967: 51). The bey appointed all judges in the court system and he could call on a Turkish military garrison to enforce his authority. As elsewhere in the Ottoman Empire, the top layer of the military and administrative bureaucracy was made up of *mamelukes*, soldier-slaves, often recruited from the Caucasus, who had no ties to the local population. Husayn Bey enjoyed such extensive freedom that he even negotiated independent treaties with Great Britain, France, Spain, Austria, and Holland. A 1710 succession law turned the bey-ship into the Husayn family's hereditary post and established a Husaynid dynasty that lasted until independence in 1956.

Despite his independent power, the bey faced meaningful constraints as he exercised it. Islamic law, or *sharia*, provided one set of constraints. It set broad but real limitations on the bey's authority through the work of the *'ulama*, the religious authorities who preached in the mosques, taught in the Quranic schools, and served as judges. Unlike the bey and his top administrators, these religious authorities generally came from the local population and maintained close ties to it. The *'ulama* often owed their positions to the bey and they never enjoyed enough independent power to openly challenge him. But their positions of moral and judicial authority allowed them to become effective organizers of popular protest if the bey abused his powers.

The bey's own economic interests provided another set of loose constraints on his power. Tunisia's urban markets, like most across the Islamic world, operated according to extensive regulations. Specialized guilds, often headed by prestigious families, made and enforced rules that governed who could practice particular trades, the quality of their work, the prices they could charge, and—very importantly—the amount of taxes they would pay. Because the bey relied on tax revenue to pay the Ottoman government in Istanbul and to run his own administration in Tunis, and because he relied on the guilds to assess and collect those taxes, he could not ignore their interests. Nor could he seize property arbitrarily or otherwise behave in ways that discouraged merchants and artisans from making money. His welfare depended on their willingness and ability to generate wealth. These considerations encouraged the bey to give the guilds a substantial degree of independence over their own affairs. These arrangements also produced a handful of wealthy families who became Tunisia's early commercial bourgeoisie.

Geography acted as a final check on the bey's power. Collecting taxes and enforcing the law posed no great challenge in the towns and villages of the Sahel and the north. Flat terrain, sedentary populations, mild climate, and proximity to Tunis made it easy to dispatch troops to these areas. This was not the case in the central and southern portions of the country or in the mountainous northwest corner along the Algerian border. In these regions, difficult terrain, forbidding climate, and nomadic populations made direct law enforcement more difficult and costly (Moore 1965: 11). In an extension of his own relationship with Istanbul, the bey appointed chiefs, or *caids*, to collect taxes and administer the law within their particular tribes.[3] As long as they kept the peace and did not prey on settled farming communities, these tribal authorities enjoyed almost complete independence. The bey in Tunis exercised more authority over his tribal populations than did his counterparts in Algeria or Morocco, but his power was never complete and uniform across the entire country.

During the reign of Hammouda Bey (1782–1814), Tunis developed into a minor Mediterranean power thanks to trade and tribute extorted from European states through threats of piracy. This prosperity reinforced relationships that served the interests of everyone who might have been able to challenge them. The bey's government was not expected to do very much beyond collecting taxes and keeping order. Merchants, craftsmen, and religious authorities stayed out of politics, and the bey did not meddle in religious and commercial affairs beyond what was necessary to maintain his position. Tribal leaders traded tax collecting and peacekeeping duties for autonomy. In the early 1800s, however, changes began to take place inside Tunisia and out that weakened the bey's power and shifted the regional balance of economic and military power more clearly in Europe's favor. By the last quarter of the century, these changes made it impossible for Tunisia to maintain its independence.

European Competition and French "Protection"

Tunisia's ties to Europe are truly ancient. Pottery shards indicate trade with Greece as early as the fourth century BCE. Following the fall of Carthage in 146 BCE, present-day Tunisia became a Roman province. Bulla Regia, el Djem, Thuburbo Majus and other sites provide enduring evidence of Tunisia's economic and cultural links to the northern side of the Mediterranean.

By the Middle Ages, merchants based in Marseille had established regular economic ties to Tunis. These ties became more extensive after France established a consulate in Tunis in 1577 (Ling 1967: 12). Through the seventeenth and eighteenth centuries, competition intensified between European countries seeking control of markets and resources around the globe. Turkey, England and, later, Italy, provided the keenest competition to France's position in Tunisia. In this game, France tried to secure its place in Tunisia through a series of concessional treaties. In 1802, Napoleon signed a peace treaty with the bey that formally acknowledged France's privileged position there.

While French commercial influence was growing, military developments began to undermine the bey's ability to project power at home and abroad. His Turkish army corps rebelled twice, in 1811 and 1816. His sea power suffered a serious blow in 1827 when the Ottoman navy (to which the bey was obliged to contribute) lost at the Battle of Navarino during the Greek war for independence. An outbreak of the plague in 1825 added to the hardship by undermining economic activity. In this weakened state, Hussein Bey had little choice but to sign a capitulation treaty in 1829 that allowed the French consul in Tunis to try legal cases involving French citizens.

French interest and influence expanded even more after France invaded neighboring Algeria in 1830. France occupied Algeria for three basic reasons. First, like most nineteenth-century European colonial powers, France saw Algeria as a valuable source of raw materials and a market for French manufactured goods. Under the aegis of the *Compagnie d'Afrique*, powerful French business interests had built a virtual monopoly on trade with Algeria in the 1700s. By the late 1820s, however, competition from other European countries had begun to challenge French commercial supremacy. Invading Algeria and making it an official part of France helped to secure French control over Algerian resources and markets.

Second, the French monarchy wanted to punish the government in Algiers for having supported France's revolutionary government. After Napoleon's defeat, the restored monarchy ordered French merchants not to repay debts to Algerians that they had incurred while buying wheat to support the Napoleonic wars.

Third, the French government wanted additional living room. It sought land on which it could settle some portion of its population and reduce the overcrowding in Paris and other cities. This goal, more than any other, distinguished France's policy in Algeria from the policy it would pursue fifty years later in Tunisia. Algeria was not simply a colony. It was a settler colony. Algeria became an official part of France in 1848 and the French government began shipping republican workers and the unemployed to new homes across the Mediterranean. To make way for them, French authorities used a variety of methods that deprived Algerians of their land and transferred it to French settlers.[4]

This dramatic increase in the French presence in North Africa sparked concern in several capitals. In Istanbul, the loss of Algeria struck a serious blow to an already weakened Ottoman Empire. Britain, Germany, and Italy all saw the increased French presence in Algeria as a threat to their ambitions in Africa and the Mediterranean. As European powers scrambled to compensate for French gains in Algeria, mounting economic difficulties made it difficult for Tunisia to maintain its independence. Just one month after the French occupation of Algeria, the Tunisian government signed a treaty that granted France most favored nation status and strengthened the powers of European consuls to judge cases involving European citizens. This treaty expanded French influence in Tunisia in two ways. Economically, the treaty opened Tunisia to French manufactured imports that undermined many traditional urban artisans and raised the prices for goods that Tunisians used to buy from local producers. Politically, the legal concessions allowed European consuls to gather around them protected collections of Europeans, Jews, and Arabic-speaking Christians. As Abun Nasr (1987: 273) describes, the assistance of these populations, combined with threats of military force, allowed European consuls to interfere in domestic Tunisian affairs for their own benefit.

By the time Ahmed Bey came to power in 1837, Tunisia was facing multiple threats to its independence. In addition to France, Tunis also had to contend with the Ottoman government in Istanbul. In the mid-nineteenth century, the sultan implemented a series of reforms that he hoped would establish firmer control over the empire and allow his government to withstand growing European power. These reforms directly threatened the bey's long-standing independence. The French presented themselves as the bey's ally and protector against Ottoman and English encroachment, but Ahmed Bey knew that France cared only about protecting its privileged position in his country (Ling 1967: 13–14).

Managing these threats became Ahmed Bey's central challenge. In an effort to bolster his power, he implemented reforms of his own. The government established a new military academy at Bardo and invested in building a larger, more professional army. By the end of Ahmed Bey's first decade in power, Tunisia boasted a regular army of 26,000 men (Abun Nasr 1987: 274). The government outlawed slavery (under pressure from Great Britain's consul to Tunis) and tried to increase government revenue by creating tax farms in the countryside.

These reforms endowed Tunisia with a more professional military that owed its primary allegiance to Tunis rather than Istanbul. But they did little to alter the country's general deterioration. Encouraged by his finance minister, Mustafa Khaznadar, Ahmed Bey embarked on a costly building program which, in addition to the costs of the military and administrative reforms, pushed Tunisia deeper into debt. Unscrupulous tax farmers; uncertain weather; and additional bouts of drought, cholera, and typhus all conspired against the efforts to boost agricultural production and to extract tax revenue from it. When Ahmed Bey felt compelled to send 4,000 troops to fight with the Ottomans in the Crimean War, he had to sell his household jewels to equip them (ibid.: 274).

Ahmed's successor, Mohammed Bey, proved an even less capable leader. He frustrated European consuls by overturning the abolition of slavery and by administering his own, very arbitrary, system of justice that threatened the security of non-Tunisians. He also threatened their economic interests by continuing to tolerate Mustafa Khaznadar's corrupt and spendthrift ways. Concerned about the security of their investments and their citizens, the British and French consuls pressured Mohammed Bey to accept reforms that would provide additional protection. Adopted in September, 1857, the *Ahd al-'Aman* (Security Pact) affirmed the security of persons and property, established the legal equality under the law of Tunisians and non-Tunisians, and gave Europeans the right to acquire property.

Combined with the deepening debt, these reforms—particularly the right to acquire property—made it easier for European interests to extend their reach into Tunisia's economy. They also encouraged influential Tunisians to press the bey for a constitution—*dustur* in Arabic—that would create an institutionalized check on his power. This document, promulgated in 1860 by Mohammed's successor, Mohammed es-Sadok Bey, became the Arab world's first constitution.[5] It affirmed the beylical office as the hereditary head of state. But it also called for a sixty-member Supreme Council with substantial power. Ministers would be accountable to it; it could control taxation and expenditure; it could appoint and dismiss high officials.

The constitution stood for only four years. The French and other European governments did not like it because the Supreme Council complicated their relations with the bey. They also did not like the idea of their citizens being subject to Tunisian law. This violated the older beylical concession that allowed foreign consuls to handle cases involving their citizens. Mohammed es-Sadok certainly did not like this check on his power, but he retained the authority to appoint the members of the Supreme Council. Consequently, the Council never functioned as its proponents hoped it would. To the relief of some and the great frustration of others, the government suspended the constitution in 1864. In that same year, a powerful revolt united the towns and tribes of the Sahel against Mohammed es-Sadok's decision to double the poll tax in order to pay some of the country's mounting debt.[6] In 1866, the Tunisian government asked the Rothschild banking house for 115 million francs to pay off the country's foreign debt and provide additional revenue for current operations. They refused (ibid.: 281–2).

Tunisia's deepening economic and political crises generated a complex challenge for European governments. On the one hand, France, Britain, and Italy shared a common concern for their considerable investments in Tunisia. France, in particular, had invested heavily in railroads, ports, phosphate mines, and agricultural production. Economic collapse and civil unrest served none of these governments' interests. To avert such a crisis, they created an International Financial Commission in 1869 to oversee Tunisia's budget (Ling 1967: 17–18).

On the other hand, each power was deeply suspicious of the others and anxious to enhance its own influence in the region. While France consolidated its hold on Algeria, Britain was gaining influence in Egypt. Italy was getting more deeply invested in Cyrenaica (Libya). Although France was the dominant economic presence in Tunisia, Italians made up the largest European population in the country. Increasingly, Paris came to see Tunisia as a vulnerable buffer between Algeria and its competitors to the East.

In 1878, Britain, France, and Germany tried to manage their Mediterranean competition at the Congress of Berlin. Germany's representative, Otto von Bismarck, suggested that Germany and Britain recognize France's preeminent interest in Tunisia. They pledged not to intervene if France ever decided to claim and occupy Tunisia as a French possession. In return, Britain hoped that France would recognize a comparable British preeminence in the eastern Mediterranean. For his part, Bismarck hoped to divert French attention and resources towards Africa and away from Europe. In the diplomatic spirit of the day, all of this was kept secret from the Ottomans since it amounted to a carving up of their empire (Ling 1967: 24; Pakenham 1991: 109–22).

Though pleased to have a free hand in Tunisia, the French government remained hesitant to use it. Many officials suspected that Bismarck wanted France to get bogged down in Africa and to lose any lingering interest in avenging the loss of Alsace-Lorraine to Germany in the Franco-Prussian War. More importantly, France feared a repeat of its experience in Algeria. After landing in 1830, French forces spent the next forty years putting down a succession of rebellions against their occupation. The last and strongest of these uprisings collapsed only seven years before the Congress of Berlin, so the memory remained fresh. Tunisia mattered to France primarily as a buffer between Algeria and Italy's position in Cyrenaica. As long as nothing happened in Tunisia that could threaten France's hold on Algeria, most French politicians had no interest in another costly military campaign and occupation.

But this was not to be. By 1880, France controlled Tunisia's rail and telegraph lines and subsidized the shipping lines between Tunis and Marseille, Malta, and Tripoli. France had established a bank that offered low-interest loans to encourage the growth of French agriculture and industry. One company had already purchased and begun investing in a tract of farmland between Tunis and Sousse that covered 1,000 square miles. France had also pressed the bey for the rights to build a new port at Tunis and for French citizens to invest in mining companies that covered a considerable portion of the country's agricultural lands.

Such extensive investments made it virtually impossible for France not to intervene directly in Tunisia's deepening economic and political crisis. Powerful interests that benefited from Tunisian government spending had thwarted the International Financial Commission's effort to impose greater financial discipline. Smuggling robbed the government of customs revenues while drought killed off cattle, sheep, and funds that the government would have raised from livestock taxes. As it became increasingly difficult for the Commission to make payments on the government's bonds, administrators began to suspect that protecting French investments would require more direct involvement. In early 1880, the French consul in Tunis, Adolphe-François de Botmiliau, lamented that, "A last attempt is made in this moment to save this country by the financial commission. If it fails, we would have to be forcibly called upon to occupy Tunisia and this will be a troublesome extremity for us" (Ling 1967: 18).

Economic hardship was not the only threat. Italy felt that Britain, France, and Germany ignored Italian interests in Tunisia. Despite the large number of Italians in Tunisia and their contributions to its development, Britain, France, and Germany had not invited Italy to the Congress of Berlin. When the Italian government purchased a small rail line connecting Tunis with one of its northern suburbs, some French colonialists called for an intervention to prevent Italy from "snatch[ing] Tunisia from under their noses" (Pakenham 1991: 109).

Economic crisis and colonial competition might have provoked an eventual French invasion. But it was unrest along the Tunisia-Algeria border that turned Botmiliau's "troublesome extremity" into a necessity in the spring of 1881. Governments in Tunis had rarely been able to exercise meaningful authority along the mountainous border. For most of the previous decade, tribes had raided at will across the border into Algeria. They had even attacked some French ships. These raids had sparked criticism that the bey was as incapable of managing his population as he was of managing the economy. In late March, 1881, several hundred Khroumir tribesmen rode into Algeria. A combined Franco-Algerian force expelled the raiders, but the French government felt that the time had come to clean out the mountains. Forces marched into the border region, then kept moving eastward. The French occupied Bizerte and then turned south towards Tunis. The bey and the Ottoman government in Istanbul called for help but received none. France was simply exercising the option that Britain and Germany had given it three years earlier. On May 12, 1881, Mohammed es-Sadok signed the Treaty of Bardo giving France substantial control over Tunisia.

Protectorate Tunisia

The colonial period casts a very long shadow across the portions of Africa and Asia that came under European rule in the eighteenth and nineteenth centuries. The economic dynamics of colonialism are well known. European powers exploited developing regions as sources of cheap raw materials, cheap labor, and captive markets for manufactured exports. These practices undermined traditional artisans, pushed native farmers off the best agricultural lands, and created powerful local elites who—like the economy—depended more on their ties to Europe than on ties to their own populations. These conditions generated powerful grievances and spawned national liberation movements across the developing world in the middle decades of the twentieth century.

Beneath these very general dynamics, however, European colonialism was not a single, homogeneous thing. European governments desired different countries for different reasons. Colonial methods reflected these differing goals as well as the particular economic, political, and social characteristics of the societies they wished to rule. Understanding these differences is vital to any understanding of post-independence politics. In so many cases, the composition of the new governments, their philosophies and methods, the institutions they created to wield power—all of these things were shaped powerfully by the ways in which the nationalist movements organized themselves and made choices about how to struggle for independence. The movements and methods, in turn, were conditioned heavily by the nature of the colonial order they sought to overthrow. Who profited and suffered under colonial rule? Who emerged as the principal spokespersons and organizers for the nationalist cause? Did nationalists come together quickly and easily in a single organization, or did factions compete with one another for control of the movement? How did the various constituencies in the nationalist movement maintain their alliance? How did the nature of colonial rule make some strategies more feasible or attractive than others? Answers to these questions explain how colonialism shaped the organizations and individuals who stepped into power at independence.

North Africa offers a particularly interesting place to study these processes. The three core Maghrebi countries—Tunisia, Algeria, and Morocco—share a French colonial heritage. In all three cases, French rule generated nationalist movements that took solid organizational shape after the First World War, became more broad-based and aggressive in the 1930s and 1940s, and won national independence in the late 1950s and early 1960s.

Through this common tapestry, however, run some very distinctive threads. French colonialism in the Maghreb reflected France's particular interests in each country and the specific social, economic, and political realities it faced in those countries. Consequently, French colonialism shaped Maghrebi societies in different ways and generated different kinds of nationalist responses. In Algeria, France's destructive colonization policies combined with local political dynamics to create a deeply divided nationalist movement. The National Liberation Front (FLN) ultimately emerged as the preeminent organization that waged a bloody eight-year war for independence and then had to consolidate power over a deeply divided and wounded society. Like Tunisia, but later (1912), Morocco became a French protectorate. A nationalist party, the Istiqlal, developed in the 1940s. But Morocco, unlike Algeria or Tunisia, maintained a monarchy with substantial power. The Istiqlal negotiated Morocco's independence in conjunction, and sometimes in conflict, with a king who cared primarily about maintaining the monarchy.[7] The competition between the king and the other components of the nationalist movement dominated post-independence politics.

As noted earlier, France's goals in Tunisia were essentially negative. France cared primarily about what it did *not* want to see happen there. It did not want any other European power to lay hands on Tunisia. But it also did not want to create another settler colony like Algeria. Paul Cambon, France's first Resident General in Tunis, argued that France served its interests best by simply allowing the bey to govern Tunisia for it. After all, the French needed little from the Tunisian government beyond its traditional tasks—collecting taxes and keeping order. As long as France controlled Tunisia's foreign and defense policy, and as long as French administrators wielded ultimate power behind the throne, the bey's administration could provide the public face for France's presence in Tunisia. Instead of loading Tunisia with settlers, destroying its government, and provoking widespread unrest, the French presented themselves as Tunisia's "protectors". France would fend off voracious European colonialists while the bey put his financial and administrative palace back in order.

The basic terms of the French Protectorate were spelled out in the 1883 Treaty of La Marsa. Tunisians kept their citizenship, their schools, their guilds, even their own courts for most matters. The bey's government and army remained in place and maintained sovereign authority over a range of domestic matters.

Behind this façade of independence, however, the treaty gave France ultimate power in Tunisia. The French Resident General controlled Tunisia's budget and served as the bey's supervisor and as Tunisia's foreign minister. He ruled the country "through the bey if he cooperated and without him if he occasionally tried to oppose his will to that of the French government" (Rudebeck 1969: 27). Similar supervisors stood behind the prime minister and other top Tunisian officials. The commander of French forces in Tunisia served as Tunisia's war minister. The treaty also required the bey's government to implement whatever administrative, judicial, and financial reforms its French supervisors recommended. The Tunisian government could not take out additional loans without French approval (Kraiem 1976: 15–16; Ling 1967: 50–2).

These reforms did more than put Tunisia under French control. They also "retained, strengthened, and extended the bureaucratic administration of the local state" (Anderson 1986: 9). The central government gained new power to appoint local authorities and to make them dependent on Tunis for their salaries. The Protectorate administration established municipal governments and improved roads and railways. Together, these measures made it much easier for the central government to reach beyond Tunis and to shape developments across the country. By strengthening existing institutions, the French undermined the autonomy of local authorities without destroying them and tipped the balance of power in the central government's favor. Tunis became the country's capital in a more meaningful way than ever before (Ling 1967: 52–62).

It is important to point out that these reforms added to an important centralizing dynamic already under way in Tunisia. This dynamic involved the most important economic resource in nineteenth-century Tunisia—land. Traditionally, a variety of tenure systems had governed land use and ownership in Tunisia. *'Arsh* was collectively owned tribal land. *Melk* was a kind of individual tenure that resembled Western-style ownership. *Habous* was land held as an endowment to support a family (private *habous*) or to support a religious or charitable institution such as a school, an orphanage, or a saint's shrine (public *habous*).[8] In some of Tunisia's grain-growing regions, there was an additional form of tenure called *hanshir*. *Hanshir* involved dual-tenure, shared between the user of the land and those who provided security for the cultivators.

Over the course of the late nineteenth century, large quantities of *hanshir* and *habous* lands were transferred to private property, usually owned by the beylical government or by absentee urban landlords. The government confiscated large quantities of tribal land as punishment for the 1864 rebellion. Urban *'ulama* took over additional *habous* lands previously held for the support of local saint's shrines.

Norma Salem describes this privatization and centralization of land ownership as "the greatest social change of the nineteenth century in Tunisia" (1984: 35). Once the French took over the beylical government, land owned by the bey essentially became land owned by the French. And land owned by absentee urban elites was much easier for French interests to buy or rent.

This experience of uninterrupted state-building and progressive centralization marks an important difference between Tunisia and many other colonized countries. In many cases, including Algeria, colonialism destroyed local political and economic institutions. Bloody rebellions against the colonial order created additional chaos. At independence, new governments faced the daunting task of constructing new economic and political institutions and of agreeing on the principles to guide them. This building process often generated deep and bitter divisions at the very time that new governments needed to maintain unity. Since Tunisia avoided this kind of profound disruption of its central governing institutions, the new government would not have to create a whole new order atop the rubble of the old one. This would be a great boon to the country's post-independence development.

The Origins of Tunisian Nationalism

France's occupation of Tunisia did not spark great opposition. Several individuals who opposed the Protectorate chose voluntary exile in other Arab countries. The tribes calculated that they would lose any open conflict with the French. France also helped to mute opposition by presenting itself in non-threatening terms, as a sort of tutor or partner in the modernization process. France would help Tunisia to develop socially, economically, and politically in ways that would benefit both countries. That rhetoric, combined with France's commitment to sustaining traditional institutions, helped to placate Tunisia's educated and traditional elite. The former saw France as a valuable partner in their own effort to reform Tunisian society. The latter understood that as long as they were willing to work within the parameters of French policy, they could hold influential positions.

But this absence of rebellion, and the fact that France's policies in Tunisia were not as destructive as its policies in Algeria, did not make the Protectorate a mere inconvenience. Indeed, its policies bear direct responsibility for the progressive impoverishment of much of the Tunisian population in the late nineteenth and early twentieth centuries.

In the 1880s and 1890s, the Protectorate used a range of measures to gain control of Tunisia's best agricultural land. While it simply confiscated some land, the law became the government's primary tool. The Protectorate passed a new land law in 1885 that called for the survey and registration of land holdings. In a country where much of the land was held collectively, the new law meant that large tracts of land now belonged to the individual in whose name it was registered. Thus, it also meant that large numbers of people lost legal access to land. Additional measures allowed non-Muslims to rent land and used Tunisian state revenues to finance newly arrived colonists.

The first foreign buyers of land in Tunisia were large finance companies, not individual settlers. Between 1882–92, fifty companies bought some 443,000 hectares from Tunisian landowners (Salem 1984: 36). In the 1890s, however, the Protectorate became more interested in encouraging more settlers. France still did not want to turn Tunisia into a settler colony like Algeria. But with Italian influence growing in Cyrenaica to the east, Protectorate authorities became concerned that Tunisia's own large Italian population might become an internal source of instability. Additional French settlers would help to counter an effort to enhance Italian influence in Tunisia.[9]

Thus, in 1892, Protectorate authorities began the official colonization of the "state domains"—lands that had been under beylical control, confiscated tribal lands, and *habous* lands. French officials distributed these lands to individual colonists with easy financing. In 1897, the Protectorate established a colonization fund that would buy land for settlers. The following year, a new rule required the administrators of habous lands to provide 2,000 hectares of land each year for sale on easy terms. Beginning in 1913, a series of measures forced many peasants onto reservations. In 1919, the *Commission de Colonisation* began confiscating more *habous* lands for sale to colonists (ibid.: 38; Abun Nasr 1987: 357). Between 1897–1922, individual colonists took over an additional 400,000–500,000 hectares (Abun Nasr 1987: 294–5; Salem 1984: 36; Ling 1967: 62–7).[10]

These policies did not bring nearly as many individual settlers into Tunisia as Algeria. As late as 1936, the French population in Tunisia numbered 108,000 (Abun Nasr, 1987: 357). But they did displace a large number of Tunisians. Many rural Tunisians farmed under *khammes* contracts. Landowners provided the land, the seed, and the tools to work them. They usually gave their *khammes* workers some wheat, barley, clothing, and olive oil at the beginning of each month. At harvest, the farmer received one-fifth of the product. Because this generally was not enough to support a family, the *khammes* worker had to borrow additional money from the landlord. As a result, debt bound many peasants to the land and the landowner. When new regulations made more land available for private purchase, peasants never had the means to buy it (Ling 1967: 70–1). Consequently, many peasants lost their places on the land when new dry-farming techniques and mechanized agriculture decreased the need for human labor.

By the end of the First World War, "almost one million hectares of the best Tunisian land were in the hands of Europeans and hundreds of thousands of Tunisians had been thrown off the land without any alternative employment" (Salem 1984: 37; Micaud *et al.* 1964: 15–16).[11] They had no alternative employment because the flood of French manufactured goods put many traditional artisans out of business and made it impossible for any indigenous Tunisian industry to develop. Those who did find jobs in the cities received less pay than French or Italian workers who did the same work (Ling 1967: 77). The result was a steady rise in rural poverty, urban migration, unemployment, and—perhaps most importantly—awareness of inequality.

In contrast to what was happening in most sectors of the economy, education was one sphere in which French policies generated beneficial effects for Tunisians. In the late 1800s, the Protectorate opened new opportunities for bright young Tunisians to receive a French education in Tunis and in France. The Protectorate presented these opportunities as evidence of their commitment to a modernizing partnership with Tunisia. They hoped to create a cadre of interlocutors between France and the Tunisian people, a group of people who had been inculcated with French values but who spoke the language of and maintained ties to their native culture. In Tunis, Sadiki College (established in 1875) and Lycée Carnot (established in 1882) became the most influential of the institutions that provided these educations. Many of the best graduates of these schools went on to university education in France.

These opportunities did expose Tunisian students to French values. But instead of using the education to facilitate French domination, many of these students turned the language and values back on the colonizers. These schools, in fact, produced the young people who became the leaders of Tunisia's nationalist movement.

The first organized criticism of the Protectorate emerged in 1906–7. Under the leadership of Bechir Sfar and Ali Bach Hamba, French-educated Tunisians began to argue that France was not living up to its own commitments. Known as the Young Tunisians, the group was not "nationalist" in the strict sense of the term. It did not advocate complete independence. Indeed, the Young Tunisians believed that French values could help to modernize Tunisian society, to free it from the hobbling constraints of "irrational" tradition. But if the French meant what they said when they described the Protectorate as a sort of tutorial, then they had to provide educated Tunisians with more opportunities to step into meaningful leadership roles. Protectorate reforms had created a more centralized state and created new educational opportunities. Giving educated Tunisians greater access to positions in this more centralized state became the Young Tunisians' central demand. Arabophone students in the more traditional Islamic curriculum at Tunis's Zaytouna University leveled similar criticisms at the government. This frustration began to find a voice with the establishment of the Khalduniya, an institution that provided modern, secular educations to Zaytouna students. In this way, discontent over the lack of professional opportunities under French rule became a bridge linking the Francophone and Arabophone members of Tunisia's rising educated elite.

In 1911–12, two outbursts of popular frustration led to the Young Tunisians' demise. In November, 1911 a large group of Tunisians clashed with police when the expansion of a quarry threatened to encroach on the Djellaz cemetery in Tunis. A few months later, Tunisian tramworkers went on strike to demand equal pay and an end to the practice of hiring Italian drivers.[12] These clashes reflected popular frustration more than a concerted nationalist strategy. The Young Tunisians supported these expressions of discontent, but they played no role in organizing them. They could not, in part, because they did not constitute an organized party. As one of the nationalist movement's leading historians describes it, "[t]he Young Tunisian movement was, in reality, a group of people with diverse opinions who developed no hierarchy or discipline" (Kraiem 1976: 147).

Additionally, the Young Tunisians did not organize popular protest—or even talk very much about pay inequality, rising inflation, deepening rural poverty or other material issues—because of their own traditional and bourgeois backgrounds. Their concerns and their legalistic approach reflected their emphasis on reforms that would create new opportunities for Tunisia's elite. Nevertheless, French authorities took advantage of the Djellaz and tramworkers protests to deport or jail the Young Tunisian leadership, shut down its newspaper, *Le Tunisien*, and impose a state of martial law that remained in place until 1921.[13] This repression, followed by the outbreak of the First World War, forced Tunisian nationalism into dormancy for the rest of the decade.

The end of the war breathed new life into Tunisian nationalism. Woodrow Wilson's commitment to national self-determination, embodied in the League of Nations, reenergized activists who had been repressed by colonial powers during the war or who had made a strategic decision to put their work on hold. Some 63,000 Tunisians had served in the French army during the war (Abun Nasr 1987: 354). Many believed that this service earned Tunisians the right to a serious conversation about their relationship with France. Additionally, two French decisions in 1919 helped to fuel Tunisian frustration. First, the Protectorate announced plans to begin confiscating more *habous* lands for colonization. Second, the French government established the *tiers colonial*, a pay scale that paid French civil servants one-third more than a Tunisian holding the same job (Anderson 1986: 148). These decisions helped to forge an alliance between secular and clerical elites who were increasingly disgruntled by the inequities of French rule. It became clearer to them that the Protectorate served only to "protect" French interests.

In 1919, Abdelaziz Taalbi pulled these two elements together in a new organization called the Destour Party. As noted earlier, *dustur* is the Arabic word for "constitution". The name reveals much about the party's background and program. Like the Young Tunisians, and much like the Wafd Party that developed at the same time in Egypt, the Destour drew heavily from Tunisia's traditional elite—large landowning families and bourgeois and religious families in Tunis. Many of them enjoyed longstanding ties to the bey and received an education that emphasized law or Islamic studies. But unlike their predecessors, the Destourians were less enchanted by the idea of a partnership with France. By the early 1920s it was clear that the Protectorate would not treat members of Tunisia's elite as equals. Modernization of the Protectorate administration further eroded the bey's authority and gave more power to French civil servants. While more Tunisians received an education that qualified them for civil service positions, the opportunities available to them continued to shrink. Similarly, Tunisia's traditional religious elites felt threatened by plans to develop private religious endowments that would undermine their influence.

Harkening back to Tunisia's brief experience with constitutional government in the early 1860s, the Destour pressed for reforms that would give Tunisia's elite more institutionalized political power. The core demands called on France to establish an elected deliberative assembly to which the government would be accountable. They also called for a separation of executive, judicial, and legislative power; expanded educational opportunities; and equal access to civil service jobs.

The Destour made its case primarily through newspaper articles and delegations to Paris. These efforts produced only limited reforms but the party never pressed its case more aggressively. In part, this moderation reflected a fear that France would decide to simply destroy the party and annex Tunisia as it had Algeria. Throughout the 1920s, French authorities jailed or exiled

Destour leaders who became too strident. But the Destour's moderation also reflected its conservative elitism. The party demanded reforms that would allow traditional elites to expand their power. The party expressed little interest in reforms that would alter Tunisia's basic social and political hierarchy. Consequently, the Destour's platform remained exclusively political and legalistic. The leadership's mistrust of the masses prevented it from mobilizing a broad, popular movement behind a program that addressed the socio-economic issues that concerned most Tunisians (Kraiem 1996: 202).

As economic conditions worsened over the course of the 1920s, this ideological and strategic conservatism progressively alienated the Destour from Tunisian society. Outbursts of spontaneous unrest became more frequent, but the party never participated in them or provided any leadership. The Destour supported Tunisian workers when they formed their own trade union in 1924 because French unions did not treat them as equals. But the party refused to support the new union's strike campaign and stood by while authorities rounded up Tunisian labor leaders. Despite deepening Tunisian dissatisfaction, the Destour never tried to unite intellectuals, traditional elites, workers, students, and farmers behind a coherent strategy.

By the late 1920s, repression and political isolation had driven the Destour into a corner. Lacking a popular base, and having lost many of their leaders to exile or prison, party officials decided to lay low until the environment changed in ways that allowed them to be more effective. The international depression in the early 1930s helped tremendously in this regard. But worsening economic conditions alone did not revive Tunisia's nationalist movement. The resurgence came about because new political actors arrived on the scene with the will to do what the Destour would not.

Habib Bourguiba and the Neo-Destour

Most contemporary scholars are deeply skeptical of "great man history"— explaining the complex development of whole countries, societies, or time periods through the ideas and actions of individual leaders. No matter how strongly one may reject the study of history through great lives, it is impossible to separate Tunisia's modern development from the life and work of one man—Habib Bourguiba.

Like many of the young men who took over Tunisia's nationalist movement in the 1930s, Bourguiba was born in the Sahel.[14] He took advantage of the new educational opportunities that opened to Tunisians in the early twentieth century and attended school at the Lycée Carnot and Sadiki College in Tunis. He then studied law in Paris.

Bourguiba returned to Tunis in 1928, on the eve of important changes for the nationalist movement and for the country as a whole. Over the course of the 1920s, the Destour had established new cells in the interior, particularly in the Sahel. This growth did not involve any substantial shift in the party's strategy. But it did draw in a considerable number of young men from backgrounds that differed dramatically from the established Destour leadership. In addition to the fact that they came from the provinces, the newer members came from middle-class families rather than from the traditional commercial and landed elite. They were the sons of provincial landowners and small businessmen who took advantage of new educational opportunities to become lawyers, teachers, salaried employees, and low-level government bureaucrats.

This combination of provincial, middle-class backgrounds with European-style educations produced activists with a more populist and aggressive outlook than the traditional Destour leaders. Younger activists showed greater concern for the daily economic challenges that confronted most Tunisians. Years of fruitless petitions and newspaper articles convinced them that the Protectorate would never treat Tunisians as equals. Complete independence was the only way to ensure justice and to improve the lives of average Tunisians. The Depression created a larger audience of Tunisians who were receptive to this kind of populist nationalism. Bourguiba and his allies argued that the party should take advantage of this environment to build a broad-based movement that united all Tunisians in a single, disciplined organization (Kraiem 1996: 203; Anderson 1986: 167–77).

This more aggressive nationalism generated a serious conflict within the Destour. Established party leaders feared that a more populist movement would seek more than independence. It might also reorder Tunisia's established social and political hierarchy in ways that undermined their power and privilege. Many Destour leaders who believed passionately in independence could not fathom a government run by the sons of small farmers and petty shopkeepers. Others argued that a mass movement and a more militant strategy would only invite French repression. The crackdown on the labor movement proved the Protectorate's willingness to repress militant nationalism.

Younger activists made their case in the pages of *L'Action tunisienne*, a newspaper that Bourguiba and his allies established in 1932. They succeeded in winning seats on the Destour's executive committee in 1933, but concluded that they could not move the conservatives to support a more aggressive and populist strategy. They would have to break with the party and start their own. That decision led to Bourguiba's barnstorming campaign to win over rank and file Destourians in early 1934. In town after town, he denied rumors that he and his supporters were communists or hotheads whose confrontational style would invite a police crackdown and destroy the nationalist movement. He explained how a broad-based movement could unify Tunisians of all regions and classes behind a careful strategy of sustained pressure that would minimize open confrontation, withstand whatever repression might come, and win independence in stages over a prolonged period of time. By March, Bourguiba had built enough support to establish a new party, the Neo-Destour.

The creation of the Neo-Destour only intensified the contest for control of the nationalist movement. When the new party increased its marches and protests to demonstrate its growing strength, Protectorate authorities arrested Bourguiba and shipped him and seven of his colleagues to a prison on the edge of the Sahara. The Neo-Destour won a brief respite when French voters elected Leon Blum's Popular Front government in 1937. The new government criticized hardline policies and pledged to forge a new partnership with Tunisians in the struggle against underdevelopment. In this spirit, the Popular Front freed Bourguiba and applied more progressive social legislation in Tunisia. Instead of eroding Tunisian nationalism, however, these reforms simply created a less repressive environment and made it easier for Bourguiba and his allies to wrest control of the movement from what came to be known as the Old Destour. By the end of the year, the Neo-Destour had recruited some 28,000 members in 432 branches across the country (Moore 1965: 108).

Conditions changed again when the Popular Front government fell in 1938. The new government returned to a harder line against nationalist activity. When demonstrations in front of the French Residence turned violent in April 1938, Protectorate authorities outlawed the Neo-Destour and arrested Bourguiba again. Unlike previous crackdowns, however, this one did not force the movement into dormancy. By the late 1930s, the Neo-Destour could sustain its campaign of strikes and sabotage even while Bourguiba was in jail because it had developed two important assets—an organization and a strategy (Ling 1967: 123).

Until his final years in power, Habib Bourguiba owed much of his success to a potent combination of clear-eyed pragmatism, a healthy sense of his own historical significance, and powerful personal charisma. The first quality gave him a keen ability to weigh balances of power, to evaluate political probabilities, and to see consequences that others did not. The second gave him the courage—some would call it hubris—to make decisions that flew in the face of conventional wisdom and popular opinion. The last quality made him a compelling dramatic actor who could reach beyond the political elite and make his case directly to the Tunisian people.

These qualities showed through clearly in the strategy that the Neo-Destour crafted in the late 1930s. Despite his unwavering commitment to independence, Bourguiba was utterly pragmatic about the means to that end. At the Neo-Destour's second congress in 1937, Bourguiba suggested that countries like Tunisia could win independence in one of three ways: they could wage a violent revolution; they could help another power defeat their colonial overlord; or they could work for a gradual transition to independence through steadily mounting pressure at home and from the international community. At a time when many nationalists clamored for armed revolt, Bourguiba argued that a gradual transition was Tunisia's only option. Tunisia simply did not possess the human and material resources to sustain a prolonged rebellion. Supporting another power against France would simply trade one master for another.

Additionally, Bourguiba understood that Tunisia was a small, relatively resource-poor country. French capital had done much to modernize the country's economy and infrastructure. In order for that development to continue, French aid and investment would have to continue, as well. That investment, in turn, would come only if Tunisia maintained good relations with France. Launching an armed rebellion or supporting another power would antagonize France and undermine Tunisia's long-term development interests. Tunisian nationalists needed to strike to a delicate balance. They needed to win independence while doing as little damage as possible to Franco-Tunisian relations.

These considerations shaped Bourguiba's position during the Second World War. Operating on the assumption that "my enemy's enemy is my friend", many nationalists across the Arab world supported Nazi Germany. A German victory, they reckoned, would break the British and French empires. In the early years of the war, when the tide ran in Germany's favor, that seemed like a good bet. But as early as 1942, and even while he sat in a French prison, Bourguiba penned the following prescient analysis to the Neo-Destour's director, Habib Thameur:

> Germany will not and cannot win the war. Between the Russian and Anglo-Saxon giants, which control the seas and have infinite industrial capacities, Germany will be crushed as in the jaws of a vice. I order you and our activists to establish relations with the Gaullist French forces and to coordinate clandestine action with them. Our support should be unconditional. This is a matter of life and death for Tunisia.
>
> (quoted in Belkhodja 1998: 14)

While the Neo-Destour continued to expand its organization during the war, Bourguiba was perfectly willing to delay the active push for independence in order to preserve French interests.

Winning independence in stages required an organization that mobilized a broad coalition of interests and deployed its energies in a very calculated way. A peaceful transition did not mean one without violence or bloodshed. It simply meant that tactics such as strikes, arson, assassination, and sabotage should never become ends in themselves. They were tools that the party should use carefully to encourage France to keep negotiating steps towards independence without provoking reprisals or alienating Tunisia's allies in France and elsewhere.

To sustain broad support, the Neo-Destour operated as "extensive patron–client networks" (Anderson 1986: 174). As noted earlier, the Depression of the 1930s took a heavy toll on Tunisians of all classes and regions. The party exploited this shared hardship to bring together constituencies that previously had little to do with one another behind the simple proposition that independence was vital to everyone's improvement. Independence, in turn, required the unified effort to all Tunisians. In this way, the Neo-Destour built nationalist support by appealing to pragmatic self-interest as well as to patriotism.

This broad coalition allowed the Neo-Destour to draw on a diverse range of assets. Business owners provided the funds for leaflets, automobiles, aid to striking workers, the unemployed, and indigent peasants. Students and workers organized nationalist unions that could disrupt schools and strategic portions of the economy. Religious authorities legitimized the nationalist cause and lent the use of mosques and local religious brotherhoods for meetings. Peasants and rural communities organized guerrilla cells whose attacks helped to ratchet up the pressure whenever French authorities became recalcitrant.

While Bourguiba clearly served as the preeminent leader and strategist within this complex organization—the *combattant suprême*, as he came to be known—he did not direct every aspect of its operation. Indeed, much of the party's strength derived from the cadre of highly skilled leaders who served as Bourguiba's lieutenants—Ahmed Ben Youssef, Farhat Hached, Ahmed Tlili, Habib Achour, Salah Ben Youssef, to name just a few. Many of these men went on to play critical roles in Tunisia's post-independence development. Most of them experienced difficult periods in their relationship with the man who saw himself as the incarnation of the Tunisian people and the most important shaper of its fate. From the late 1930s to the late 1940s, however, their leadership allowed the party to continue functioning during the multiple and extended periods when Bourguiba was either in jail or out of the country.

The Push for Independence

When Bourguiba returned to Tunisia in early 1943, the political environment had changed considerably—but not as much as he had hoped. His prediction about the course of the war proved accurate. Allied forces were on the verge of taking North Africa and would soon launch their assault on Fortress Europe. The occupation of Tunisia by Axis and Allied forces had weakened France's hold on the country and given the Neo-Destour more freedom to build its organization. This shift in the balance of power between France and the nationalists, along with signals that the United States would support them, convinced Neo-Destour leaders that the time was ripe for a renewed push.

Bourguiba hoped that France would reward his wartime loyalty by showing more willingness to discuss progress towards independence. He planned to press for internal autonomy as a prelude to full independence. Instead, French authorities forbade him to engage in political activity and required him to remain within the city of Tunis. Hobbled by these constraints, Bourguiba decided to focus his energies outside the country. He secretly fled Tunisia in March, 1945, and spent the next four years trying—in vain—to rally support across the Arab world, Europe, and the United States. Other

Arab nationalists cared primarily about their own struggles. The US and most Europeans focused on reconstruction and the beginning of the Cold War.

In September 1949, French authorities allowed Bourguiba back into Tunisia. They hoped that his return would split the nationalist movement. During his four years abroad, leadership of the Neo-Destour passed to the party's Secretary General, Salah Ben Youssef. Scion of a prosperous merchant family on the island of Djerba, Ben Youssef enjoyed close ties to Tunisia's traditional commercial and religious elite. While Bourguiba represented a Tunisian identity that was more "Mediterranean" and more heavily influenced by European ideas and culture, Ben Youssef represented an identity that was more attuned to the Arab East and to traditional Islamic culture. He was also drawn to the kind of pan-Arab nationalism that was gathering steam in Egypt, Syria, Iraq and other portions of the Arab world. During Bourguiba's absence, Ben Youssef had loaded the Neo-Destour with activists who shared his views. This created a conflict between "Youssefists", who wanted to adopt a more militant strategy as part of the broader pan-Arab effort to expel European colonial powers, and "Bourguibists", who advocated a more moderate strategy based on a negotiated transition to independence. French authorities hoped that Bourguiba's return would fuel this conflict and split the Neo-Destour (Toumi 1989: 18–26).

Through the early 1950s, Bourguibists and Youssefists maintained an uneasy truce. Both camps realized the importance of maintaining unity. Bourguiba's shift to more aggressive tactics also helped to paper over tensions within the party. He knew that more militant methods raised the risk of a French crackdown. But lower levels of militancy had failed to move France and he had been unable to mobilize international pressure on Paris. If he did not turn up the heat at home, the nationalist movement would stall and he would be swept aside by the Youssefists. More militant tactics would placate some of his Youssefist critics; increase pressure on the Protectorate administration in Tunis; and attract more international attention, especially from the US, the French Left, and the new United Nations. Based on this logic, Bourguiba called for a new wave of guerrilla activity in the countryside and of student and worker strikes in the cities and in key sectors of the economy. The years between 1949–54 became the most violent in Tunisia's struggle for independence.

Organized labor became Bourguiba's most important ally in the early phase of this campaign. After two unsuccessful efforts in the 1920s and 1930s, Tunisian workers finally established their own labor union, the *Union Générale Tunisienne du Travail* (UGTT), in 1946. French authorities who had opposed earlier attempts to create a specifically Tunisian union now saw it as a useful tool for pulling Tunisian workers away from French unions that had fallen under communist control. Unlike the Old Destour, the Neo-Destour saw the union as an asset rather than a threat. The UGTT provided well-organized cadres in the public administration and in key sectors of the economy—public works, the ports, the railways, and the phosphate mines. As more of these workers became convinced that independence was a prerequisite to real improvement in their pay and working conditions, they became more willing to move political demands to the top of their agenda and to serve as a striking arm for the Neo-Destour. They also were inclined to support Bourguiba's more progressive wing of the party rather than the more conservative Youssefist wing. In return, Bourguiba provided the UGTT with skilled leadership and financial support.

By 1951, the UGTT had become the most important organization in the country after the Neo-Destour. It boasted nearly 100,000 members and its strike campaign had become "a veritable social war against the state" in support of the Neo-Destour's demands for internal autonomy and negotiations leading to independence (Ben Hamida 1989: 101–2). The UGTT also built ties to American and European trade union organizations that helped to publicize the nationalist cause. One observer described Farhat Hached, the UGTT's secretary general, as "the kingpin of Tunisian nationalism, the activist master of the most disciplined troops, the best conceived doctrine and the strongest alliances" (Meric 1973: 292). When Protectorate authorities arrested most of the Neo-Destour's leadership in January, 1952, Bourguiba asked Hached to direct the nationalist movement in his absence. Hached served in that capacity for nearly a year before French terrorists assassinated him for opposing reforms that would grant Tunisia co-sovereignty rather than internal autonomy or independence.

Hached's death and the subsequent crackdown on the UGTT leadership dealt a serious blow to the nationalist cause. Nationalist leaders decided that large strikes and demonstrations had become too risky. They also feared that these tactics would tire the merchants and workers who paid dearly for them. Instead, the movement shifted to guerrilla action as the primary tool for pressing France to make concessions.

By itself, this surge in nationalist protest probably would not have convinced France to grant Tunisian independence. But the unrest inside Tunisia coincided with developments outside the country that prompted France to reconsider its policy. At the broadest level, the political and economic challenges involved in recovering from the Second World War made it difficult for Britain and France to sustain pre-war commitments to many of their colonial holdings. As noted earlier, France occupied Tunisia primarily to defend Algeria from other European powers. By the early 1950s the risk of losing Algeria to another European power had disappeared. But the risk of losing Algeria to the Algerians had begun to increase dramatically. The economic and political incentives to hold on to Algeria far outweighed those for Tunisia. Faced with more violent resistance in Algeria and Morocco, and bogged down in Indochina, letting go of Tunisia made increasing sense. Serious recommendations for granting Tunisia internal autonomy circulated at least as early as 1952.

The Cold War also played a role in the politics of Tunisian independence. Bourguiba's willingness to support Gaullist forces against Germany and its

Vichy allies during the Second World War never paid the dividends that he hoped to receive. As the Cold War intensified, his willingness to side with the West proved a bit more profitable. By the mid-1950s, the scramble for allies in the developing world, and the rise of the non-aligned movement, made the US and its allies more willing to support Tunisian independence in return for Bourguiba's commitment to an explicitly pro-Western foreign policy.

On July 31, 1954, Prime Minister Pierre Mendès France landed at Tunis-Carthage airport and announced France's willingness to grant Tunisia internal autonomy. Bourguiba had been in Paris until June 1, carefully managing the final discussions. On August 7, a new government, selected by the Neo-Destour, began negotiating the terms of a new Franco-Tunisian relationship. These negotiations marked the first of Tunisia's final steps to independence. But they also opened one of the most difficult chapters in Tunisia's modern history.

The Youssefist faction within the Neo-Destour openly criticized the internal autonomy talks. Salah Ben Youssef argued that Tunisia should press for full independence and should do so as part of a pan-Maghreb effort to win independence for Tunisia, Algeria, and Morocco. In part, this position reflected strategic and philosophical differences between the Bourguibist and Youssefist factions. Ben Youssef believed that the Maghreb countries would win independence more quickly if they launched a unified revolt against French rule. This commitment lay at the heart of the Movement for the Liberation of North Africa, an organization whose 1947 charter stated that none of the signatory nationalist parties would pursue a separate peace with France. The Neo-Destour signed the charter and Ben Youssef believed that the party should abide by it as a matter of both principle and pragmatic national interest. This commitment to a multi-national armed strategy also drew Ben Youssef closer to Gamal Abd al-Nasser's pan-Arabism (Toumi 1989: 18–23).

Bourguiba's time in Egypt had soured him on Nasser and pan-Arabism. Perhaps because of his own charisma and ambition, Bourguiba was skeptical of others with the same traits. He saw Nasser as a self-aggrandizing egomaniac who manipulated pan-Arab rhetoric and other political leaders to bolster Egypt's interests and his own stature. In his own mind, Bourguiba was honest enough to make it clear that he was a Tunisian nationalist first and foremost. If it made pragmatic sense for Tunisia to pursue its own course towards independence, then that is what Tunisia should do.

Politics also played an important role in the mounting conflict between Bourguibists and Youssefists. Both men had built supporting coalitions that reflected differing socio-economic interests. Bourguiba depended heavily on the support of organized labor and others who supported a more progressive, left-leaning program. Ben Youssef enjoyed stronger support from religious leaders, from members of Tunisia's commercial and landed classes, and from those with strong pan-Maghreb or pan-Arab sentiments. These coalitions functioned as patron–client networks based on reciprocity. Competing leaders would reward supporters with access to jobs and other benefits after their faction took control of the party and the newly independent state. Once independence became virtually inevitable, factions that had remained unified for the sake of pressuring France began to think more about ensuring their own ascendancy.

The tension between the two factions increased after Bourguiba's supporters took control of the party in 1955. By early 1956, assassinations and other acts of violence between the two factions made it seem likely that Tunisia would erupt into a civil war even before it became fully independent. Ben Youssef fled the country in late January, 1956, a week after a bomb was discovered in the building that housed his offices. Two months later, on March 20, Bourguiba decided that the best way to end the escalating conflict was to break off the internal autonomy talks and simply proclaim Tunisia's full independence.

Looking Backward, and Forward

Compared to many countries in the Arab world and beyond, Tunisia's struggle for independence was a relatively bloodless and orderly affair. The French Protectorate played an important role in producing this outcome. Defending French interests in Tunisia did not require extensive colonial settlement or other measures that destroyed Tunisia's traditional social and political order. France could accomplish its goals by expanding and manipulating a process of state formation that began during the late Ottoman period.

This is not to say that the Protectorate did not create serious dislocations and injustices for Tunisians. Indeed, the inequities generated by the colonial order provided the tinder on which nationalist leaders struck their spark. But compared to Algeria, for example, where settler colonialism and official integration into France dispossessed thousands of Algerians and tore down indigenous social and political structures, the disruptions created by colonial rule in Tunisia were much less extensive. This contrast helps us to understand why civil servants, rather than guerrilla fighters, played the most critical role in Tunisia's nationalist movement. Tunisia's struggle did not involve a fight over land or between two fundamentally different political orders. Rather, it was largely a struggle over who would staff and lead the organs of a central government that had developed steadily for more than a century.

The Bourguiba–Ben Youssef struggle notwithstanding, Tunisia also entered independence with a fairly unified political elite that enjoyed extensive connections to a broad cross-section of the population. Politics within the Neo-Destour certainly involved personal animosities, regional rivalries, and differences of opinion about how the party should wage the struggle and prepare to govern. But these conflicts took place within the context of a single mass party. This relative unity saved Tunisia from the fratricidal bloodletting and the crippling political gridlock that plagued many countries after independence had been won.

At the same time, however, it is important to recognize that the Neo-Destour's emphasis on national unity also shaped Tunisia's development in less healthy ways. Because the party needed to sustain a broad base that included landowners and peasants, owners and workers, the religious and the secular, it avoided elaborating a detailed program or philosophy. This ambiguity provided post-independence officials with valuable maneuvering room. But it also opened the door to bitter disputes within the party and society at large over the principles that should guide Tunisia's development.

The politics of national unity made it difficult for Tunisians to manage these disputes. The party's claim to represent all Tunisians, combined with Bourguiba's feeling that he was the only man capable of leading the country, produced a majoritarian view of politics that left no room for "loyal opposition". It turned all of the young country's political disputes into personal conflicts within the party. It also left unanswered the most basic question about the role of national organizations such as the worker and student unions—were they tools of the party or independent representatives of their constituents' interests? Many of the tensions that these limitations and ambiguities generated in a country undergoing rapid change continue to shape Tunisian politics today.

2 Authoritarianism and stability in Tunisian politics

A 1982 book on North African politics included a chapter entitled, "Tunisia: A Single-Party System Holds Change in Abeyance" (Stone 1982). Many would say that this title remains as appropriate today as then. Tunisia's ruling party is no longer its only party. More social and political organizations function without official ties to the government. More women participate in politics at all levels than ever before. But looking back over the past five decades, one is struck primarily by how little the substance of Tunisian politics has changed, by how often the same issues have recurred, and by how often Tunisia's rulers have used similar strategies to deal with those issues.

This stability has been a mixed blessing. The absence of chronic military conflict or domestic unrest has allowed the government to invest heavily in economic and social development. Tunisia never developed the kind of bloated and parasitic military that has devoured scarce resources in many Arab countries. Stability also has allowed Tunisian and foreign investors to make important choices that they likely would not have made in a more uncertain environment.

On the negative side of the ledger, Tunisia remains a deeply authoritarian place. It continues to be dominated by a president who faces no serious institutional constraint and who directs a ruling party that remains virtually indistinguishable from the organs of the state. That party enjoys such strong advantages that it does not need to be the only legal party in order to remain dominant. The rules of the political game make it virtually impossible for other parties, alone or in coalition, to replace it. The government regularly violates a broad range of individual and collective rights. When Tunisia's rulers have supported political reforms, they have crafted them in ways that create the impression of change more than its reality. If Tunisians have never changed president or ruling party through violence, neither have they changed them through the ballot box. They are not likely to do so any time soon.

Tunisia's post-independence political history falls into three reasonably clear time periods. The first period corresponds to the first decade after independence. Between 1956 and the late 1960s, politics was dominated by the Neo-Destour's evolution from a mass-based nationalist movement into an authoritarian ruling party. The second period, the late 1960s through the mid-1980s, witnessed steadily growing opposition to the party and to Bourguiba. For much of this period, the most vocal and effective opposition came from leftists on university campuses and in the trade union movement. Toward the end of this period, however, the Islamist movement emerged as the most serious threat to the regime. In November 1987, the fear of a civil war between the government and the Islamists prompted Zine al-Abidine Ben Ali, who served as both Interior Minister and Prime Minister, to organize a bloodless coup and to replace Bourguiba as president. Ben Ali's rule marks the third period, though it has lasted long enough to generate identifiable phases within it.

The First Decade: Mass Movement to Authoritarian Party

Although pragmatism was a defining characteristic of Bourguiba's politics, he also believed that he was uniquely qualified—even destined—to become the architect of modern Tunisia. He believed that Tunisia remained trapped by traditional attachments to families, clans, villages, and regions, attach-ments that stunted the development of a modern, national identity. Building a modern state, and modern citizens to go with it, required a strong leader with a unique vision. In his own mind, only he possessed the charisma, the intelligence, and the modern perspective required to make this happen.

This unwavering certainty about his destiny sustained Bourguiba in times of crisis. But, as one of his close associates points out, it also "made him slide naturally towards authoritarianism and a certain cynicism in his relations with others ... Throughout his long reign, Bourguiba worked to make others adopt his model, to inculcate them with his values" (Belkhodja 1998: 19). This ego and sense of destiny would have made Bourguiba jeal-ous of his power under any set of circumstances. The conditions that existed at independence only strengthened this impulse.

Tunisia in 1956 was a very unsettled place. The Neo-Destour had won independence through a protracted bargaining process rather than a dra-matic victory. Unemployment remained near 30 percent. Bourguiba alien-ated traditional interests by abolishing *habous* lands and *sharïa* courts; by basing his power on an alliance with the left wing of the Neo-Destour; and by championing a Personal Status Code that outlawed polygamy, defined marriage as a voluntary contract that required the bride's consent, set a minimum age for marriage, and gave women divorce rights. Deep personal and philosophical conflicts within the Neo-Destour threatened to plunge the country into civil war. Under the slogan "the rifle instead of the ballot box", Youssefists boycotted the first legislative elections, held just five days after independence. They assassinated some party officials who refused their strong advice to do likewise. The boycott, supported by many Old Destourians, did not prevent Bourguiba's supporters from winning all of the seats in the new National Assembly. But the low turnout in Tunis, Jerba, and elsewhere made it clear that Bourguiba still faced considerable opposition in critical quarters (Toumi 1989: 27–9).

He also had to contend with one of the most difficult and enduring issues in modern Tunisian politics—relations between the ruling party and the trade union. The UGTT had been one of Bourguiba's most important allies in the struggle against both the French and the Youssefists.[1] Union leaders supported the internal autonomy accords. They also moderated wage demands and strike activity in order to help Bourguiba win over Tunisian and French business owners. To maintain the UGTT's support, Bourguiba had committed himself to its economic program: centralized economic planning, nationalization of major industries, and land reform that would divide large landholdings into cooperatives. After the first legislative elections in March, 1956, Bourguiba allocated nearly two dozen of the ninety seats in the National Assembly to the union. The UGTT's general secretary, Ahmed Ben Salah, became the leader of the left aisle within the Assembly and headed its powerful legal and constitutional committees. Four members of the UGTT's top leadership received ministerial appointments.

This was precisely the kind of political involvement that many UGTT leaders sought. They understood that holding together a broad coalition had forced Bourguiba to avoid clear ideological pronouncements. But they also believed that this effort to be all things to all people had prevented the Neo-Destour from developing a coherent social and economic development program. Now that independence was won, union leaders believed that they were uniquely qualified to help the government design just such a plan. The union had prepared the most thorough analysis ever conducted of the country's economic and social situation. Armed with this study and the political clout they had earned during the independence struggle, UGTT leaders hoped to endow the Neo-Destour and the government with a socialist development program. The union's 1956 congress passed resolutions calling for a planned economy, nationalization of key industries, agricultural cooperatives, a single ministry that would oversee the planning process, and a guaranteed right to strike (Moore 1965: 64–7). The union also called for the UGTT's "organic participation" in the life of the party.

These propositions sent shock waves through the Neo-Destour. Conservative members of the party had always been suspicious of Bourguiba's populist rhetoric. But they counted on him as a bulwark against the socialists and communists. They held their noses and accepted his earlier commitments to the UGTT as a political necessity. But they would not allow the UGTT to turn the Neo-Destour into a labor party. The UGTT's powerful place in the new government and its open call to invest the party with a socialist ideology posed too great a threat to their interests.

It threatened Bourguiba's interests, too. His alliance with the union reflected shared interests more than a shared philosophy. The union's socialism smacked too much of class conflict for a leader committed to a broad, cross-class coalition. It also smacked too much of ambition. Ben Salah, the UGTT's secretary general, was the driving force behind the union's philosophy and strategy. He was an ambitious young man who had risen very quickly in the union and the party. Bourguiba was not prepared to turn "his" party over to anyone. Nor was he prepared to allow any ideological commitment to limit his freedom of movement. Ben Salah had to go. But he had to go in a way that did not alienate the UGTT.

Ironically, Bourguiba's own methods complicated the task of eliminating Ben Salah. Because they wanted the UGTT to maintain control over the rank and file, Bourguiba and other party leaders had supported Ben Salah's efforts to centralize power and to ensure that top union officials could intervene in local and regional unions. Ben Salah had extended his control over the union apparatus so thoroughly that internal competitors could not unseat him at the ballot box. Consequently, Bourguiba resorted to a divide and conquer strategy that he would use repeatedly over the next three decades against the union, opposition political parties, and other civil society organizations.

Habib Achour was a UGTT pioneer from Sfax and a long-time Destourian with close personal ties to Bourguiba. He enjoyed a reputation as a rough and tumble rabble-rouser. Achour led some of the most combative strikes during the independence struggle. His tough-talking style made him a favorite with agricultural laborers, manual workers, and the unemployed. But these qualities did not make him many friends among the party's landed and commercial constituencies. Nor did they sit well with the educated civil servants who controlled the UGTT under Ben Salah.

Achour had hoped to become the UGTT's general secretary in 1954. But the civil servants who took control of the UGTT after Farhat Hached's assassination had worked hard on behalf of Ben Salah's selection. Achour resented Ben Salah's rapid rise, and Bourguiba exploited this resentment by suggesting that the government would support a breakaway union. Fortified by the party's money and press, Achour and his supporters pulled out of the UGTT and established the Tunisian Labor Union (UTT). The UTT presented itself as a true union, one that cared about representing workers rather than getting involved in party politics.

It became clear that the UTT was a ploy to eliminate Ben Salah when it issued three demands as conditions for rejoining the UGTT: Ben Salah had to step down, union officials could not hold ministerial positions, the two unions had to come together in a "unity congress" that involved equal numbers of delegates from both organizations. The first condition would eliminate Ben Salah, the second would reduce the union's role in government, the third would give Achour and his allies a chance to enhance their power in the UGTT despite the fact that the UTT attracted relatively little rank and file support.

The two unions reunited in May 1957 on terms entirely favorable to Bourguiba's interests. The new secretary general, Ahmed Tlili, also served as the Neo-Destour's treasurer, a member of its Political Bureau, and one of Bourguiba's most trusted lieutenants. Bourguiba put Achour on the party's Political Bureau, as well, and the union put him in charge of its economic affairs. Ben Salah had been eliminated, the UGTT's two top officials had been coopted onto the party's Political Bureau, and the union's rank and file had been divided and weakened by the schism. The new union leadership rarely criticized the government's development strategy or supported strikes. Bourguiba brought Ben Salah into the government as Secretary of State for Social Affairs. He later became the architect of Tunisia's planned economy in the 1960s.[2]

Bourguiba's management of the UGTT is significant for at least two reasons. First, coopting its leadership seriously handicapped Tunisia's democratic development. The union represented a large portion of the population and it made valuable contributions to discussions about Tunisia's future. Breaking its independence robbed the country of a rich source of reflection, debate, and leadership. It also struck a fatal blow to the notion of an independent civil society.

The UGTT's experience also illustrates an important characteristic of Bourguiba's methodology. As noted earlier, encouraging schism and reunification on his terms became one of his standard methods for weakening organizations and eliminating leaders he could not control. It made much more sense to personalize conflicts and manipulate people rather than kill or exile them. The latter methods risked creating a culture of political violence that produced deep divisions, required higher levels of security spending, and created periods of instability that could alienate investors. Permanently eliminating all signs of political ambition and competition would also rob the country of some of its best political talent.

Part of Bourguiba's genius lay in his ability to play competing factions and personalities off against one another and to use promotions to pull people under his thumb. This management style kept all of the relevant players inside the party. But it also kept them off balance and allowed Bourguiba to function as the maker and breaker of careers. It personalized politics by preventing "the crystallization of personal cliques into vested interests, whether they be in the name of labor, students, business, agriculture, or even the Destour" (Moore 1966: 217–18). Opposition under Bourguiba became "a matter of individuals, who could be sent into private life to cool their heels before being recalled to service by the president" (Zartman 1988: 81).

Personalizing politics and coopting national organizations were not the only ways in which Tunisian politics became more authoritarian after independence. The new constitution also set real limits on the country's democratic potential. Over the course of 1958, Tunisian elites hotly debated a broad range of constitutional issues. In general terms, the debate pitted those who wanted to balance legislative and executive power against those— including Bourguiba—who wanted to give the executive a freer hand. An initial draft identified significant legislative powers. Over the course of the following months, however, several developments conspired to weaken these provisions. Influential advocates of a more balanced system either died or got pulled into the government. The war in Algeria, a suspension of French financial assistance, and evidence of a Youssefist plot to assassinate Bourguiba bolstered his case that the times demanded national unity under strong leadership. The final draft of the constitution, promulgated on June 1, 1959, established a presidency with wide-ranging powers, including the power to select the prime minister. Tunisians would hear a very similar argument from Bourguiba's successor in the 1990s.

The new constitution also established powerful limits on several fundamental rights and liberties. The text declared freedoms of the press, assembly, and organization. But the constitution said that all rights and liberties had to be exercised "according to the dispositions of the law". This innocuous-sounding phrase arguably has done more than any other single measure to undermine the development of effective political opposition in Tunisia. This clause gave the National Assembly the right to define exactly what each of these freedoms meant and how Tunisians could exercise them. If one party occupies all seats in the legislature, and if the president wields a strong hand over that party and legislature, then this very reasonable-sounding language puts a constitutional legal fig leaf over the president's ability to determine what citizens may say or do. The result is a system that deprives citizens of the very rights and liberties the constitution claims to provide.

For example, the 1959 constitution included the right to strike. But the National Assembly had the power to define how that right could be exercised. In 1966, faced with a deteriorating economy and rising unrest, the Assembly adopted a new labor code that defined the right to strike so narrowly that the right virtually ceased to exist despite its constitutional guarantee. Similar procedures have allowed the government to set strict limits on the freedoms of press and assembly. Rather than placing fundamental rights and liberties beyond the easy reach of legislators, the constitution provided the government with legal tools for attacking opponents.

Bourguiba's authoritarianism intensified over the course of the 1960s. In January 1963, the government banned the Tunisian Communist Party (PCT). Two months later, the Neo-Destour's national council officially declared its support for a single-party regime. Henceforth, the party and the state became indistinguishable from one another. Leaders in national organizations received posts in the party leadership. On two occasions in the early 1960s, Bourguiba and his allies intervened again in the UGTT's internal politics to replace the union's general secretary.[3] After the party changed its name to the Destourian Socialist Party (PSD) in 1964, officials began establishing party cells inside government offices, public enterprises, and national organizations. Governors became the party's representatives and enforcers for their regions. By the middle of the decade, the ruling party had become little more than a transmission belt for the government. And although the party/state had extended its tentacles into every aspect of public life, it was losing the popular support that made it such an effective nationalist movement.

This deepening authoritarianism reflected several concerns. In December 1962, security officials discovered a Youssefist plot to overthrow the government. The conspiracy included army officers and enjoyed the support of pan-Arab nationalists like Egypt's president Gamal Abd Al-Nasser. As noted earlier, Bourguiba was deeply suspicious of pan-Arabism. He believed that it was unrealistic and that it threatened Tunisia's sovereignty. But he also understood how powerful it had become in the popular imagination. If he was going to resist the most popular idea and the most powerful leader in the Arab world, he had to tighten control over his own state.

Economic issues also encouraged tighter integration between the ruling party and the state. After independence, Bourguiba opted for a market-driven economic development strategy. By the early 1960s, it had become clear that Tunisia's private sector was not willing or able to provide the engine for economic growth. The state would have to become that engine. Tunisia needed a planned economy under firm central direction. The party and the government had to work closely to mobilize resources, including popular participation, and to coordinate investments and activities across the various sectors of the economy. The Tunisian left had been pressing for this kind of development strategy since before independence. Pan-Arab nationalists also frequently used the term "socialism" to describe their state-run development strategies. Working that term into the Neo-Destour's new name would help to gain both groups' support.

In many respects, the 1960s laid the foundation for what Tunisia would become in the 1970s and 1980s. The government's investments in economic infrastructure created the bases for a more industrialized economy. Social investments expanded literacy and improved public health.

In spite of these advances and the government's efforts to eliminate political threats, two developments in the late 1960s generated new forms of opposition. In 1967, Bourguiba suffered a serious heart attack. In a country with no vice-president and no institutionalized means for selecting a successor, Bourguiba's illness became a profoundly political issue. Some party elites began to question Bourguiba's ability to lead the country. The ambitious saw his illness as the first meaningful opportunity for someone else to move into the presidency. Rival factions began to jockey for position in the event that Bourguiba died or decided to clarify how his successor would be chosen.

Economic developments added to the uncertainty. By the late 1960s, Tunisia's economy had deteriorated badly. Agricultural production fell dramatically and pushed up Tunisia's food import bill. These imports, along with the government's extensive investments in new industrial and infrastructure projects, quadrupled the country's debt over the course of the decade. The cost of living rose steadily while wages remained stagnant. Unemployment remained above 20 percent.

The economy's decline, combined with Bourguiba's, affected politics in powerful ways. As economic frustrations increased, wildcat strikes and student demonstrations broke out despite the government's efforts to coopt unions and to prevent public expressions of opposition. Some party and government officials began to see these demonstrations as strategic tools. By discreetly encouraging them, they could build alliances with workers, students, or other constituencies that might strengthen their hand in the succession game. This elite willingness to ally with social actors created additional incentives for them to increase their militancy. This dynamic would drive much of Tunisia's political unrest in the 1970s and 1980s.

The immediate target of all this scheming was Ahmed Ben Salah, the former UGTT general secretary who directed Tunisian economic policy in the 1960s. Landed and commercial interests never supported Ben Salah's policies. To many of them, he was an ambitious opportunist peddling an "imported ideology" that was ill-suited to Tunisia. The country's mounting economic difficulties seemed to prove their point. When Ben Salah announced plans to repair the economy by extending cooperatives over the entire agricultural sector in early 1969, the fierce opposition of conservative elements within the party convinced Bourguiba that Ben Salah had to go. Almost overnight, Ben Salah went from being the country's economic czar to a jailed criminal accused of mismanaging the country's economy. Bourguiba expelled him and his supporters from the government and the party. Almost as quickly, the government's economic strategy switched from "socialism" to a full-bore campaign to liberate the private sector and encourage market-driven growth. To oversee this more market-oriented strategy, Bourguiba appointed an economist, Hedi Nouira, to the prime ministership.

Through it all, Bourguiba claimed that he had been duped. The economic mess was all Ben Salah's doing. Bourguiba claimed no responsibility beyond having allowed Ben Salah to amass too much power. Some Tunisians took this reaction as further evidence that Bourguiba was not up to the task of leading the country. He had lost control of the party and the basic organs of government. Others found his response simply unbelievable. This was the man who built the Neo-Destour, the man who had carefully planned and directed every aspect of Tunisia's political life for more than two decades, the man who evaluated every decision in terms of its impact on his power. The idea that such a man had been taken in and controlled by anyone struck many Tunisians as incredible.

This perspective was especially common within Tunisia's growing leftist community. Over the course of the 1960s, frustration over authoritarian government and economic hardship mixed with anger over developments in Palestine and Tunisia's support for the US in Vietnam to boost leftist sympathies on university campuses, particularly the General Union of Tunisian Students (UGET), and in portions of the UGTT base. Faculty, student, and workers unions became collecting points for a range of leftist ideologies.

Although the government outlawed the Tunisian Communist Party in 1963, it never tried to round up its members. More influential was the Group for Tunisian Socialist Study and Action (GEAST). Known widely by the name of its journal, *Perspectives*, the semi-clandestine group reflected a range of leftist opinions. It worked to spread its ideas and to influence the activities of other organizations. Over the course of the 1970s, these activists, with the support of some elites, rebelled against the sclerotic authoritarianism that developed in the first decade after independence.

The 1970s

By 1971, Bourguiba was weaker—politically and physically—than he had ever been in his career. In an effort to appear more attentive to public grievances, he had allowed a brief period of open debate about the country's economic and political health the previous summer. Officials were shocked by the breadth and depth of public disenchantment with the government. Across the country, in the press, on radio and television, citizens seized this unparalleled opportunity to speak truth to power. An excitement swept the country, a sense that Tunisia might be on the cusp of fundamental changes that would make the government more open and responsive.

Within the PSD, a liberal wing led by Ahmed Mestiri argued that the party must seize this opportunity to reform itself and restore its credibility, particularly with young people. To do that, the party had to begin with internal changes to make itself more democratic. The liberals pressed Bourguiba to call a congress that would allow the party to start this renewal. Bourguiba consented, but he believed that much of the talk about reform was fueled more by ambition than principle. Putting an end to the succession question would put an end to the maneuvering. With that in mind, Bourguiba announced at the congress that he wanted to designate Prime Minister Nouira as his successor to the presidency.

The liberals rejected Bourguiba's succession plan. The idea that Bourguiba should be able to hand-pick his successor went against the very spirit of the reforms they advocated. Instead, the liberals passed a resolution that designated the president of the National Assembly as the official who would step into the presidency. They also passed a resolution that said that members of the party's ruling body, the Political Bureau, should be elected by party leaders rather than appointed by the president.

Bourguiba would have none of it. In his closing remarks to the party's central committee, he declared that "as long as I am alive, I will be the chief of state" (Belkhodja 1998: 121). He personally selected the members of the Political Bureau and he expelled Mestiri from the party's central committee for comments that he made to the foreign press.[4]

Over the next two years, the PSD's leadership changed significantly. A large number of party members were expelled or chose to resign. Along with the purge of Ben Salah and his followers, the expulsions and resignations of

Mestiri and other liberals robbed the PSD of some of its most experienced leaders. Into the void stepped a new generation of officials, technocrats with little experience and none of the political stature of the people who had fled or been chased out. To a greater extent than ever before, the party and the government became an inseparable promotion machine, drawing in ambitious careerists who gained and maintained their positions through loyalty to Bourguiba. Delegates to the PSD's 1974 congress easily passed resolutions designating the prime minister as Bourguiba's successor and designating Bourguiba as the party's president for life. Hedi Nouira declared before the delegates:

> The dominant feature of our political society is the indivisible character of the party and the state ... Our political system essentially revolves around the party, creator of the ruling ideology and the organizer of the masses, and the state, the instrument of organized power. This party–state symbiosis in conceiving and formulating policy should be translated in our institutions and structures.
>
> (Belkhodja 1998: 274)

Four months later, the National Assembly declared Bourguiba president of the republic for life.

While these changes helped Bourguiba to restore some measure of control over the PSD, they widened the gap between the government and an increasingly restive population. In the first half of the 1970s, good weather, healthy harvests, and strong prices for Tunisia's export commodities produced annual growth rates of 8–10 percent. This performance placed Tunisia among the top ten countries in terms of GDP growth per person. By mid-decade, however, many Tunisians had begun to express frustrations over the distribution of this growth. The government and private business owners raised wages in the early 1970s, but they did not peg wages to the cost of living. Inflation rates between 5 and 10 percent more than neutralized the effects of the wage increases. Inflation imposed a particular hardship on wage earners because prices were especially high for goods and services that consumed a larger percentage of low and middle incomes—transportation and fruits and vegetables. The wealthiest 20 percent of the population disposed of 50 percent of total household spending while the poorest 20 percent disposed of only 5.6 percent. The UGTT argued that while the real average salary for workers rose 18 percent from 1971–75, incomes for independent professionals rose 68 percent. Industrial and commercial profits rose 115 percent. Conditions for low and middle income families became even more difficult after 1975 when falling export prices and rising food imports eroded Tunisia's macroeconomic health (Union Générale Tunisienne de Travail 1977: 12–14; Ben Romdhane 1985: 28–32; J. Zouari 1993: 16).

Important social changes made more Tunisians willing to protest these grievances. Tunisia in the mid-1970s was very different from Tunisia in the late 1950s and early 1960s. Unprecedented numbers of a young people received secondary and university educations at home or in Europe. The university experience politicized them in ways that made them more inclined to protest. The growth of the public sector meant that more Tunisians worked in factories or offices with stronger, and more politicized, union organizations. Access to French media exposed Tunisians to the 1968 student and worker strikes and to the rich mix of ideas in the country that served as a cultural and political reference point for many Tunisians. These developments produced a society that was more willing to question the government, to demand that it become more responsive to the people, and to protest perceived inequities.

Mounting frustration over an out-of-touch authoritarian government and the unequal distribution of wealth provided a fertile context for a range of left and social democratic movements. In addition to the PCT and smaller, far left groups, liberal exiles and defectors from the PSD formed a new Movement of Social Democrats (MDS). The MDS played a key role in establishing the Tunisian Human Rights League (LTDH) in 1977, the oldest human rights organization in the Arab world.

A bit further to the left lay the Popular Unity Movement (MUP). Ahmed Ben Salah established the MUP in 1973, after he escaped from prison in Tunis and fled to Switzerland. The MUP provided a gathering point for Tunisians sympathetic to the ideals that inspired Ben Salah's policies in the 1960s—a communitarian socialism that emphasized the state's role in building a more unified and enlightened society. These ideals appealed to an important segment of the Tunisian intelligentsia and to the Tunisian community in Europe. The MUP's 1977 Charter of Democratic and Popular Liberties laid out basic political principles that had a powerful influence on the general political debate in Tunisia.[5]

The PCT, the MDS, and the MUP were not legal in the mid-1970s. Even if they had been, they lacked the resources to build broad support across the country. By and large, they were parlor societies made up of elites in Tunis. The government tolerated them as relatively harmless release valves for intellectual frustration. In order to build popular opposition to the government, these movements needed to work through some other organization with resources and a national structure.

This quest for allies placed the UGTT in the middle of the intensifying conflict between the government and the opposition. As rank and file worker unrest increased, activists with political commitments beyond the union movement tried to use it for explicitly political purposes. Increasingly, union discussions of grievances and demands went beyond worker issues and took up demands for political reform. By organizing wildcat strikes, activists hoped to force the UGTT leadership to distance itself from the government and to make the union a battering ram for political, as well as economic, change.

Bourguiba and Prime Minister Hedi Nouira hoped to use those same union leaders to secure social peace. By involving them in a new wage bargaining process with the government and leaders of the private business community, Bourguiba and Nouira hoped to quell rising social protest and undermine the left. Unveiled with much fanfare in 1973, this new relationship would unite government, labor, and capital as "social partners" in a "contract for progress".

The strategy failed miserably. Once again, Bourguiba had chosen to deal with a complex social and political conflict by treating it as a highly personalized affair. The new bargaining relationship was supposed to work because labor and business leaders had been coopted onto the party's political bureau and because of the very long personal relationship between Bourguiba, Nouira, and the UGTT's general secretary, Habib Achour. At the end of the day, these three old comrades would get together and work out whatever needed to be resolved. Beneath the rhetoric about a new, more institutionalized relationship between "social partners", the "contract for progress" was nothing more than an agreement between three or four individuals. The whole arrangement rested on political self-interest and personal ties rather than on a systematic approach to socio-economic challenges. Consequently, it did nothing to address the root causes of rising unrest.

Through the mid-1970s, student and worker strikes became the primary manifestation of the country's deepening crisis. The government came down hard on the student union early in the decade, but the repression did little to stem the rising tide of protest. In 1977, the unrest spread beyond campuses and factories. In October, a worker strike at a state-owned textile plant in Ksar Hellal—the birthplace of the Neo-Destour—escalated into a three-day general uprising. Three months later, on January 26, 1978, the UGTT called Tunisia's first general strike since independence. It, too, turned into a more general uprising as thousands took to the streets, attacking ministries and businesses in the heart of Tunis. "Black Thursday" marked the first time that Tunisian security forces fired on their own citizens. Non-governmental sources estimated 200 dead and 1,000 wounded. Two years later, on the second anniversary of Black Thursday, a group of Tunisian commandos attacked the southern town of Gafsa, the capital of Tunisia's disaffected phosphate mining region. Calling themselves the Tunisian Liberation Army, and acting with Libyan support, the rebels' communiqué described their attack as "the starting point for a movement that will liberate the country from the PSD's dictatorship and from neo-colonial domination" (Belkhodja 1998: 244).

The Gafsa revolt shocked the political establishment. It was one thing to have Tunisians in the streets. It was another thing entirely to have a self-styled "liberation army" on the attack with Libyan support. It suggested that others in the region believed that the government had lost so much support that they could find allies inside the country to do their bidding.

After a decade of escalating unrest, this fear finally moved Bourguiba to consider significant political reform. He named a new prime minister, Mohamed Mzali, whose principal task was to calm tensions and reach out to the opposition. The government released a large number of trade unionists and others who had been arrested after the Black Thursday strike. Bourguiba also repealed the expulsions of the liberals who had been driven from the PSD in the early 1970s. Some of them returned to the fold and received important ministerial appointments. In preparation for new parliamentary elections in 1981, the government lifted the ban on the PCT and declared its willingness to legalize parties besides the PSD.

These initiatives not only marked the beginning of the government's willingness to allow other parties to participate in elections. They also marked the beginning of its effort to use electoral reform to control which parties could participate, to divide the opposition and coopt some of its leaders, and to craft measures that created the appearance of reform while preventing any serious threat to the president or the ruling party.

If the government offered to legalize opposition parties, it did not make the process easy. It granted temporary authorization for the well-known "parties in waiting" (the MDS, the MUP, and the PCT) to enter lists of candidates. In order to become fully legal after the elections, however, a party had to receive at least 5 percent of the national vote. This posed a formidable challenge in a country where opposition parties had no money and where the media and the entire political structure, from the capital to the smallest village, had been controlled by one party for thirty years.

In the event, the parties never got a fair chance to cross even this daunting threshold. As the elections drew near, Bourguiba became concerned that the PSD might actually lose, particularly in the capital city where the MDS put forward a compelling list of candidates. At the last minute, Bourguiba and other top officials intervened to ensure a complete PSD victory. Party officials manipulated the voter rolls, intimidated opposition observers at polling places, and falsified the vote count. According to the official results, the PSD received 94.6 percent of the vote. The MDS received only 3.2 percent. The MUP and the PCT both received less than 1 percent.

Bourguiba saved the elections for the PSD, but the whole experience was an embarrassing disaster. Everyone, including the foreign press, knew that the government had gotten cold feet and fouled the results. "Democracy" was a fine thing as long as it restored popular support for Bourguiba and the PSD. But when it looked as though voters might actually take advantage of the opportunity to vote for another party, Bourguiba pulled the plug. Just as he had ten years earlier when he rejected the liberals' effort to reform the PSD, Bourguiba frittered away another opportunity to save the country— and himself—from another difficult decade.

Economic Crisis and the Rise of the Islamists

In the early 1970s, an economic boom allowed the Tunisian government to try to buy social peace. While a small handful of intellectuals and ambitious elites clamored for reform, the government tried to prevent them from building broad support by providing generous wage increases and consumer subsidies.

By the early 1980s, economic and social conditions in Tunisia were much more difficult than they had been a decade earlier. Over 20 percent of the population still lived below the official poverty line. Two-thirds of all males and three-quarters of all females with high school educations could not find jobs. Inflation hovered around 10 percent. While 17 percent of Tunisian families lived in one-room apartments in 1975, that figure had climbed to 26 percent by 1980. Some 21 percent of Tunis's growing population lived in crowded shantytowns on the city's periphery (Ben Dhiaf 1982: 584; J. Zouari 1993: 16; Zghal 1984: 34). By 1980, the government fund that subsidized bread and other basic consumer commodities ran a deficit in excess of 100 million dinars. Poor harvests forced the government to import large amounts of wheat to cover basic consumption needs. These imports made up only one part of a growing trade imbalance. Imports rose 12.5 percent annually while exports grew only 7.5 percent. Tunisian authorities also worried that Spain and Portugal's entry into the European Economic Community in the near future would further challenge Tunisia's vital citrus and olive oil exports. Beyond the trade imbalance and rising food subsidies, inefficient state-owned enterprises constituted another costly drain on the economy. Economic conditions only worsened as the decade progressed.

Once again, the government tried to use the UGTT to reduce social tensions. The government allowed the union to rebuild its organization and to elect a more independent leadership. The government also gave union leaders new opportunities to shape the government's economic and social policies. Prime Minister Mzali was trying to keep the peace so that he could keep his job and the right to succeed Bourguiba. He was also trying to implicate the UGTT in the painful economic decisions that he knew he had to make. As a foundation for this relationship, Mzali negotiated an agreement that traded a wage increase for the union's commitment to refrain from new wage demands and strikes for an extended period of time.

Economics and politics conspired to undermine this truce. Steady economic deterioration quickly stripped the purchasing power from the wage increases. It also made employers more resistant to union activity in their plants and shops. Leftist activists within the UGTT resented the agreement their leaders had accepted. To them, the agreement did not simply leave workers exposed to unpredictable increases in inflation. It also meant that they could not use strikes as tools for pressuring the government for political reform. Their refusal to abide by the deal convinced Mzali that the UGTT had broken its truce. He came to see the union as a threat to the country's stability—and to his own ambitions. In 1984–85, Mzali waged a fierce campaign that split the union, jailed its leaders, and took over its headquarters. Mzali's crackdown ended the UGTT's reign as "the sole political mediator between the government and the nation" (Toumi 1989: 183).

It also opened the way for a new mediator. In the early 1970s, the Tunisian government—like others in the region—had quietly supported an organization called the Association for the Safeguard of the Quran (ASQ). The ASQ emphasized the Arabic language and Islamic values as cornerstones of Tunisian identity. The group had no explicit political agenda, but it did criticize the leftist organizations that bedeviled the government from the campuses and unions. Bourguiba and his allies "hesitated to see rivals in the ranks of those who criticized Marxism with a conviction that equaled their own" (Burgat and Dowell 1993: 190). The government's crackdown on the student union in the early 1970s opened up new possibilities for the ASQ on campuses. While the government battled the UGTT, the ASQ quietly expanded its student following.[6]

Relations between the government and the Islamists became less cordial after 1979. The Iranian revolution demonstrated how a movement inspired by Islamic values could take up socio-economic grievances that traditionally had been monopolized by the left. Just as the crackdown on the student union had opened the universities to the Islamists in the early 1970s, the repression against the UGTT in 1978 created a new void on the political landscape. Following Black Thursday, a more politicized Islamist movement stepped into that void. The movement began organizing demonstrations and criticizing the government's secular authoritarianism. Government officials responded by calling the Islamists opportunists who exploited religion for political gain or communists masquerading behind beards.

When Bourguiba and Mzali allowed other parties to organize for the 1981 elections, a group calling itself the Islamic Tendency Movement (MTI) applied for recognition. Led by Sheikh Rachid al-Ghannouchi, the MTI rejected violence and pledged its support for democratic, multi-party political institutions. These commitments and its emphasis on adapting Islamic principles to a modern context earned the MTI a strong following at home and abroad.

Despite these pledges, the government quickly rejected the MTI's application. At that point, Mzali was not interested in doing business with the MTI. In his mind, the UGTT remained the country's most influential organization. The key to social peace, and to his presidential aspirations, lay in an alliance with the left rather than the Islamists. In July 1981, the government arrested 61 MTI activists and charged them with forming an illegal organization, defaming the president, and publishing false news. Mzali kept up this harsh campaign for the next two years.

By 1984, however, the political situation had changed. In January of that year, the country exploded in "bread riots" after the government tried to reduce its spending by eliminating subsidies on several basic consumer goods.[7] The government's alliance with the UGTT was falling apart and its campaign against the MTI was not working. In spite of the government's repression, the MTI had expanded its base and rebuilt its organization on campuses and in poor neighborhoods. This turn of events reshaped Mzali's political calculations. Perhaps the Islamists were the new, rising social force. If so, then he needed to cultivate them. Opening a dialogue with the MTI also might draw it out of the clandestine corners that radicalized it. Thus, Mzali concluded that the time had come to deliver "a stick to the left and a carrot to the right" (Burgat and Dowell 1993: 198). He released Islamists from jail, allowed their publications to reappear and began talking with MTI leaders. In these discussions, many believe that Mzali explicitly agreed to legalize the MTI if it supported his effort to maintain the prime ministership and succeed Bourguiba.

The MTI took full advantage of its new freedom. It increased contacts with other opposition parties and civil society organizations. It issued joint communiqués with them and supported the UGTT in the face of Mzali's crackdown in 1984–85. It worked to develop a presence in other organizations while it continued to build its own. By 1985, "the Islamists were present on all fronts" (Toumi 1989: 196).

This was not what Mzali had in mind. This rapid growth and collaboration with other organizations suggested that the MTI might not be a trustworthy ally. It might decide to use its new strength to make its own bid for power. At a time when Bourguiba's physical and mental deterioration had turned politics at the top of the government into a graceless free-for-all, Mzali could not tolerate this kind of uncertainty about the MTI's strength and intentions.

Mzali turned on the MTI savagely, but it was not enough to save him. Bourguiba sacked him in July 1986 for failing to address the mounting economic crisis and for currying favor with the opposition in order to bolster his own position. In his place Bourguiba named Rachid Sfar. Sfar was a fine economist who began implementing a structural adjustment plan negotiated with the IMF and the World Bank. But he lacked charisma and political ambition. If this was a refreshing change in a prime minister, it also meant that he lacked the influence to impose order in such a highly politicized environment.

The more important personnel change that Spring took place at the Interior Ministry. Unlike many countries in the Middle East and Africa, Tunisia never developed a highly politicized military. Bourguiba feared that a large, well-funded military could challenge his rule or limit his independence. He consistently limited the armed forces' budgets and he never appointed military officers to civilian posts. Bourguiba broke with that practice when he named Zine al-Abidine Ben Ali as Tunisia's new Interior Minister in April 1986. Ben Ali was a general who had built a career in the internal security and intelligence services. Under his direction at the

Interior Ministry, the security services increased their surveillance and harassment of union officials and leaders of the opposition parties and the human rights league. The government also banned opposition newspapers and police officers attacked some party offices.

By the late summer of 1987, Bourguiba's struggle with the Islamists had pushed Tunisia to the brink of civil war. In March, police arrested Sheikh Ghannouchi for delivering a speech in an unlicensed mosque. In protest, MTI activists organized daily, rolling demonstrations. Police would arrive at one location and the protest suddenly would break out somewhere else in the city. At the end of March, French police discovered a network involving seven Tunisians with ties to Iran. That discovery, along with explosions at four tourist hotels on the coast, provided Bourguiba with the justification for trials that he hoped would culminate in the execution of top MTI leaders. When the courts did not hand down a sufficient number of death sentences, Bourguiba demanded retrials.

This demand came amidst growing concerns about his senility. On October 2, Bourguiba promoted Ben Ali to prime minister—Tunisia's third in fifteen months. The same day, he fired a party director whom he had named just three days earlier. The new director served two weeks before Bourguiba fired him, as well. Three weeks later, Bourguiba dismissed two planning and finance officials and accused them of trying to trick him. This erratic behavior, along with his persistent call for retrials that would almost certainly produce serious civil conflict, convinced many officials that Bourguiba was no longer fit to govern.

In early November, police discovered a plot by a clandestine wing of the MTI to assassinate Bourguiba and Ben Ali if they proceeded with the retrials. Bourguiba had ordered those trials to begin by November 9. On the night of November 6–7, Ben Ali assembled seven physicians who attested to Bourguiba's inability to continue to govern. The commander of the National Guard took over the presidential palace. Tunisians awoke the next morning to a new president.[8]

Ben Ali's New Era

Ben Ali did not cut a compelling figure as a national savior. Despite his time as interior and prime ministers, he was not one of the ruling party barons. He had not spent the 1970s and 1980s building alliances and jockeying for influence. He was not charismatic; he was not a backslapper or a stirring orator. Beyond his detailed knowledge of Tunisia's security apparatus, Ben Ali simply did not appear to bring many tools to the job of being Tunisia's president. That perception turned out to be one of his most important assets during his first year in power.

Ben Ali did not want an all-out war with the Islamists in 1987. The MTI had developed a large organization with an armed, clandestine component. Even Ben Ali could not be certain of its true capabilities. In light of the general disenchantment across the country, a war with the Islamists might produce a groundswell of popular support for them and overwhelm the new government. Even if that did not happen, prolonged unrest would frighten investors, undermine Tunisia's ability to negotiate loans on favorable terms, and invite meddling from others in the region. Pulling back from the brink with the Islamists, reaching out to the secular opposition, and restoring public support for the government became Ben Ali's top priorities.

In his first year as president, Ben Ali launched a barrage of reforms and an aggressive public relations campaign. He amnestied thousands of political prisoners, including Rachid al-Ghannouchi, and commuted the death sentences handed down in the September trials to life terms in prison. He satisfied two of the opposition's long-standing demands when he abolished the state security court and the presidency for life. He invited exiled opposition leaders to return home and he met with the leaders of the MDS, the PCT, and the PUP within his first month. He relaxed the press code and eased restrictions on the formation of associations and political parties.[9] On the human rights front, the new government reformed the rules governing preventive detention, ratified the United Nations Torture Convention, and established a "de facto moratorium" on the death penalty (Waltz 1995: 36). To emphasize his commitment to democracy and the rule of law, Ben Ali pressed the PSD to change its name to the Democratic Constitutional Rally (RCD). The party would open its doors to all Tunisians, particularly the young. It would represent a new majority that could lead the country more effectively because it incorporated a wider range of views.

Ben Ali capped his first year with a National Pact, a document that laid out broad principles that would guide politics and attract as many constituencies as possible to his new "presidential majority". Unlike national pacts in other countries, Tunisia's did not institutionalize substantive economic and political bargains (Anderson 1991). But it did talk about establishing "traditions of loyal competition" and "a legitimate right to differ which signifies neither sedition nor division". It reiterated the Arabo-Islamic roots of Tunisian identity. It reaffirmed support for the Code of Personal Status, for human rights, for freedoms of opinion and association exercised within the context of the law. Sixteen political parties and organizations signed the Pact.

This emphasis on values and broad principles raises an important point about the reforms that dominated Ben Ali's first year. The language that Ben Ali used to describe the measures was as important as the measures themselves. Bourguiba talked often about "democracy", but he always did it in ways that emphasized the importance of national unity. The interests of the corporate whole took clear precedence over any individual or particular interests. Ben Ali, on the other hand, spoke the language of *liberal* democracy. He not only talked about multiple parties, competitive elections, and equal rights for women. He also talked about the rule of law and individual rights and liberties, including the right to hold and express opinions that differed from the majority or from the government.

The new government's reforms, cast in language that suggested a deeper commitment to democracy, generated real enthusiasm across the country. Ben Ali's liberal commitments seemed all the more credible because he brought so few obvious political assets to the job. Because he lacked any real constituency, opposition organizations believed that Ben Ali needed them in a way that Bourguiba never did. His reforms were not hollow gestures. They were real political currency, paid out to win their support. They had won. The Islamists were getting out of jail and joining the national debate. The government was legalizing and courting opposition parties. Several leading opposition figures and intellectuals joined the RCD and accepted positions in the new government because it was implementing the very reforms that they had always demanded.[10]

Therein lay the problem. For years, Tunisia's opposition had pressed the government for expanded freedoms to organize, to express their own views, and to participate in the electoral process. Regardless of whatever else each of them believed or wanted, all parties and organizations needed these basic freedoms in order to work towards their other goals. If this set of demands suggested a healthy consensus on fundamental values, it also suggested a monotonous uniformity. In the minds of most Tunisians, they all said the same thing. Now the government was saying it, too. Ben Ali had taken the wind out of their sails by coopting their message and some of their best leaders. While he preached the virtues of pluralism and democracy, the new president had deftly sapped the opposition's ability to do anything but applaud him.

Ben Ali was not building a truly competitive democracy. Rather, he was laying the foundations for what many observers began to call a "consensual democracy"—a political order that allowed a bit more freedom to express opinions and to organize within boundaries drawn and defended by the state (Limam 1989). Ben Ali described this kind of order at a November 1990 symposium on democratic transitions: "The state fixes the fundamental framework, creates the climate and provides the fundamental necessities for competition and dialogue. Civil society should accept these and oppose any acts that go against the national consensus" (Daoud 1990: 793). Reducing tensions, allowing freer—but not free—expression of opinions, and opening the ruling party to more diverse views would allow the RCD to define this new consensus. Debate might take place, but it would take place within the RCD, a party thoroughly controlled by Ben Ali. Political liberalization was a tactic that allowed the party to gather information about opinions and preferences and to coopt substantial portions of the opposition. The whole process was designed to help Ben Ali and the RCD rule more effectively, not to create a process that might turn them out of office on election day.

While the new government was talking about democracy, it was also setting real limits on its exercise. After a slate of independent candidates won the December 1987 municipal elections in Ksar Hellal, RCD officials intervened to ensure their party's victory in elections the following month for parliamentary vacancies in Tunis, Zaghouan, Gafsa, and Monastir. While the government allowed a host of new newspapers and magazines to appear, it also began signaling limits to writers and editors. In December 1988, for example, the government seized copies of *Al-Mawqaf*, the newspaper of the Progressive Socialist Rally (RSP) after it published an article on Tunisia's nonlegal movements and parties. A week later, the government seized copies of *Réalités*, a popular news weekly, for an editorial that criticized the lack of judicial independence (Waltz 1995: 38–9).

These seizures marked the beginning of an insidious new form of press control. The government legalized many new publications and declared its respect for freedom of the press. It even provided funding to help some newspapers. But then security forces would jail a journalist or confiscate copies of publications because they wrote or published an article that did not sit well with the president. Because the government never laid out an explicit list of topics that journalists could not touch, they never knew exactly when they would cross the line into forbidden territory. This uncertainty forced members of the press to err on the side of caution when making decisions about their stories. The result was a wooden, self-censored press even though the government appeared to be relaxing the formal restrictions on it.

On the human rights front, the international community praised Ben Ali for limiting the practice of holding suspects without charge or trial. But the new law still allowed the government to hold prisoners without charge or trial for up to eighteen months (ibid.: 38)

More than anything else, however, it was the new electoral laws that made it clear that Tunisia's politics would not change as much as many hoped. Tunisia's opposition parties made three specific demands. First, they wanted Ben Ali to move forward the date for new elections. Under the electoral calendar in place when Ben Ali seized power, legislative elections would not take place until 1991. The opposition parties argued that if Ben Ali wanted Tunisians and outside observers to take his democratic rhetoric seriously, he could not allow the country to spend the first four years of his rule with a single-party legislature elected under the old regime.

Second, the opposition wanted Ben Ali to do more than simply make it easier for other parties to become legal. They pressed him to adopt additional reforms that would give them a meaningful chance of winning. Existing law established a majority list voting system and petition require-ments for all candidates. These rules made it virtually impossible for oppos-ition parties to field candidates across the whole country and to win seats in the Assembly. Even if a party could gather a sufficient number of signatures, the rules gave all the seats in a given district to the party that won a majority of the vote in that district. Thus, a party that won 48 percent of the vote in a district received none of the seats allocated to that district if another party won 52 percent.

Given the RCD's national infrastructure, its privileged access to the media, and its ability to reward supporters and punish opponents, none of the opposition parties stood the slightest chance of winning seats in the National Assembly under these rules. The opposition called on the government to disentangle the state bureaucracy from the RCD, to abolish the petition requirement and to replace the majority list system with a proportional representation system that would allow them to win seats in districts in proportion to their share of the vote. The opposition also demanded freer access to television and radio. These reforms would give them a chance to enter the National Assembly despite their relatively small bases of support and their meager resources.

The third demand came from the MTI. It wanted the government to legalize their party along with the secular organizations. Its leaders worked very hard to convince Ben Ali of their democratic commitments. They praised him for removing Bourguiba and saving the country from chaos. They reiterated their rejection of violence and their commitment to democratic politics. They softened their opposition to the Code of Personal Status. They even changed the party's name to Hizb Ennahdha, the Renaissance Party, to comply with a new law forbidding party names to contain religious references. By the spring of 1989, Islamist leaders believed that they had satisfied the requirements to become a legal party.[11]

These demands put Ben Ali in a delicate position. He needed to keep the opposition on the hook, believing in his professed commitment to democratic reform. Accusations of electoral foot-dragging undermined his credibility with them. But Ben Ali remained uncertain about the opposition's strength. He also needed to keep the support of conservative elements in the RCD who opposed electoral reforms that might undermine their control of the National Assembly. Resistance to legalizing an Islamist party remained particularly fierce. MTI candidates won 85 percent of the votes cast in student elections two months after Ben Ali came to power. What if they did as well in general elections? And what if the Islamists were only masquerading as democrats? What if they used the ballot box one time to gain power and then replaced democracy with theocracy?

Hoping to satisfy all the players in this complex game, Ben Ali made a series of critical decisions. To placate the opposition, he moved the legislative elections up to April 1989. To appease the conservatives in the RCD, he supported a "new" electoral code that kept the old majority list system. In each district where it wanted to compete, a party had to put up a slate of candidates and to obtain the exclusive support of 75 voters in that district. These rules posed no difficulty for the RCD, but they worked a tremendous hardship on small, new parties that did not have national organizations and constituencies.

Ben Ali knew that the opposition parties would object to these requirements, so he suggested that all of the parties that signed the National Pact— including the Islamists—join the RCD on single lists. The RCD would cover the campaign costs and the parties would divide the seats in the National

Assembly on the basis of a predetermined formula. This system ensured that the opposition parties received some seats. Ben Ali needed that in order to maintain his democratic credibility. But it also meant that he could fix the formula in a way that guaranteed a healthy RCD majority, something he needed to placate hardliners in the party.

Ben Ali also split the difference on the question of legalizing an Islamist party. RCD opposition and his own uncertainty about the Islamists' strength would not allow him to legalize Ennahdha outright. But he did not want to exclude them from the electoral process entirely. Dangling the prospect of eventual legalization encouraged Ennahdha leaders to stay with their moderate course despite rising impatience among their rank and file. Shutting them out completely would remove these incentives for good behavior. Allowing them to participate in some fashion also would give the government an opportunity to gather information about their organization and following. Thus, Ben Ali rejected Ennahdha's bid for legalization on the grounds that it had not yet developed a substantive program as a party. But he promised to revisit the issue after the party articulated a more developed platform. In the meantime, Ennahdha could field candidates as "independents" in the April 1989 elections (Dahmani 1989).

Ben Ali's single list was a powerful temptation for the opposition parties. Fixing the distribution of seats before the vote violated the core democratic notion that ballots should determine the distribution of power. But it offered the opposition parties a guaranteed presence in the Assembly. Most of these parties remained so small that they would be hard pressed even to field candidates in more than two or three locations. Actually winning seats against the RCD would be impossible. However objectionable Ben Ali's offer might be, it might serve a greater good to break the RCD's monopoly and establish a foothold in the National Assembly.

For this reason, most opposition politicians were willing to accept Ben Ali's offer. Even Ennahdha was willing to play the game. The Islamists remained very open to the idea of long-term cooperation with Mestiri and the MDS. In the short term, however, Ben Ali's offer gave them a chance to begin building an electoral organization, to demonstrate their commitment to democracy, and to clear the way to legalization. They would not sacrifice these important goals for the MDS's immediate ambitions.

Those ambitions ultimately destroyed the prospects for a single list. The idea collapsed when the MDS's general secretary, Ahmed Mestiri, turned it down. Even though many MDS officials supported the single list idea, Mestiri argued that fixing the division of seats before the vote made a mockery of democracy. He also complained that the RCD did not give the opposition parties sufficient opportunity to shape the platform on which the single lists would run. The opposition parties simply had to fall in behind the RCD's positions.

This was Mestiri's public justification for rejecting the single list. Privately, however, many observers believed that the decision had more to do with

Mestiri's own ambitions for his party or for himself. Mestiri believed that if the Islamists could not run their own candidates, their supporters would vote for the MDS. The MDS lost these votes when Ben Ali agreed to let Islamists run as independents and when Ennahdha took the offer instead of instructing their supporters to vote for the MDS. Additionally, many Tunisians considered Mestiri the most credible opposition candidate for the presidency at some point in the future. Ben Ali's reforms and his promises of additional measures led Mestiri to believe that this point might come relatively soon. The electoral code required any presidential candidate to have the support of at least 33 deputies in the National Assembly. Ben Ali had offered to fix the distribution of seats in a way that guaranteed the opposition a presence. But he would not give the MDS 33 seats. Mestiri rejected the single list either because he believed that the MDS, the oldest and most credible secular opposition party, could win more seats on its own, or because the rejection might prompt Ben Ali to offer the MDS more seats.[12]

Mestiri's decision killed the single-list initiative. After he rejected it on grounds that it was patently undemocratic, the other opposition parties could not touch it without undermining their own credibility. They also rejected the offer, but they were furious with Mestiri for sabotaging their chance to enter the Assembly. Consequently, Tunisia's opposition parties entered the 1989 elections divided and weakened against the RCD's formidable machine.

The April 1989 elections altered Tunisian politics in two ways. First, they made it clear that "Zinestroika" would not lead to a full democratic transition. The electoral code, the questionable conduct of the voting in many areas, and the fact that the RCD won all 141 seats in the National Assembly made it clear that Ben Ali remained unable, unwilling, or both, to implement the democratic transition he had promised.

Second, the results made it clear that Ennahdha, not the MDS, was Tunisia's most popular opposition party. Nation-wide, the independent Islamist lists received just over 14 percent of the vote. In urban areas, they received more than 30 percent. The MDS received just under 4 percent; all of the other parties won less than 1 percent (Soudan and Belhassen 1989).

Bolstered by their strong showing, Ennahdha leaders called again on Ben Ali to legalize their party. They argued that if the government continued to lock them out of the legal political process in the face of such clear public support, they might not be able to control more militant segments of the rank and file. Some in the government made the same argument, but most did not. Frightened by the evidence of Ennahdha's strength, many officials urged Ben Ali to stop flirting with the Islamists and destroy them once and for all. Ben Ali's honeymoon with the opposition was over.

The End of the Honeymoon

The April 1989 vote revealed the flaws in Ben Ali's "double strategy of opening towards the secular opposition and of ideologically going around the Islamists" (Burgat and Dowell 1993: 233). The Islamists had grown too big to go around. The secular opposition was too weak to take meaningful advantage of the narrow opening that Ben Ali offered.

Ben Ali needed to shift this balance. He rejected Ennahdha's request for legalization on the grounds that several of its leaders had served jail terms longer than three months. Although Ben Ali pardoned most of these leaders, the government had not restored their right to run for public office. The government also stepped up harassment of Ennahdha activists and their families. Human rights activists reported the increasing frequency of arbitrary arrests, passport seizures, and incidents of torture. Unable to preach or organize, Sheikh Ghannouchi left Tunisia a month after the elections.

Ennahdha's more militant elements held up the government's refusal to legalize their party as proof that trading moderation for legalization would never pay off. Ali Laaridh, the movement's spokesman, accused the government of being "incapable of dialogue" and said that Ennahdha should "continue the fight because there is no longer any means of reaching an agreement with the government. Through demonstrations in the street we fight for our rights and country's" (Marouki 1990: 33). As rank and file protest intensified, Ghannouchi, now trying to direct the movement from abroad, felt compelled to toughen his own rhetoric in order to maintain his base inside Tunisia. By the time he arrived in Algiers in the summer of 1990, he had begun calling for veiling women, suppressing foreign tourism, applying Islamic law more strictly, and a popular uprising against the government. Ben Ali met this rising militancy with more intense repression.

As the conflict with the Islamists heated up, Ben Ali offered to consider some of the secular opposition's reform proposals. For their part, secular leaders believed that they could exploit the conflict between the government and Ennahdha to their advantage. They knew that the government would not go as far as they wanted without additional pressure. Their poor showing in the April elections gave them little bargaining power in their own right. But they could play on Ben Ali's fear of a united opposition front. By drawing closer to Ennahdha, they might force him to make concessions that they could not win on their own. Based on these calculations, the MDS, the PCT, the MUP, and the Tunisian Communist Workers Party (POCT) began working in the Spring of 1990 to develop a unified list of demands. They also criticized the government's repression and called on Ben Ali to legalize Ennahdha.

This heightened cooperation produced only meager results. Ben Ali agreed to reform the rules that would govern the June 1990 municipal elections. But substantial impediments still made it very difficult for opposition parties to win. Convinced that they could extract additional concessions if they played hard to get while the conflict with the Islamists escalated, most of the parties boycotted the elections.

Iraq's invasion of Kuwait in August reinforced this opposition unity. All of the parties, especially Ennahdha, saw the crisis as a valuable opportunity to increase pressure on Ben Ali. Most Tunisians felt little fondness for Saddam Hussein, but they opposed US intervention in the region more strongly. Widespread disenchantment with Ben Ali's feeble opposition to the US made it easier for the opposition to organize marches that displayed their popular support and that occasionally took up domestic issues. A demonstration–repression cycle escalated steadily through the fall of 1990 (Limam 1990: 10–11).

The Gulf crisis also aggravated the mounting tensions between moderates and militants within Ennahdha. Still trying to maintain control over an increasingly militant base inside the country, Sheikh Ghannouchi—by then living in London—voiced strong support for Iraq. Some of the movement's leaders inside Tunisia disagreed with that position. Ennahdha had long relied on financial support from conservative Gulf governments. Supporting Iraq's claim to Kuwait threatened this critical base of support.

The government encouraged these fissures and hoped that Ennahdha would destroy itself. In late December, however, Ben Ali concluded that war in the Gulf was inevitable. He feared that its outbreak would reunify Ennahdha and spark a new wave of protest. Ennahdha leaders had already lifted their long-standing ban on violence (Soudan and Gharbi 1991). If a pitched battle with Ennahdha had become inevitable, Ben Ali wanted to launch a preemptive strike. During the last week of December, security forces arrested some 200 Islamist activists.

This crackdown actually made Ennahdha more dangerous. Ghannouchi's exile and the government's repression had already frustrated communication between Ennahdha's leadership and base. The December arrests cast the movement into deeper disarray. Base cells remained largely intact, casting about for their own responses to what they saw as the government's final campaign to destroy Ennahdha. On February 17, 1991, three Islamist activists attacked an RCD office in the Bab Souika quarter of Tunis. Ennahdha leaders condemned the attack and denied that the men belonged to their movement. True or not, the government seized the incident as a pretext to launch a full-scale assault on Ennahdha. Security forces rounded up thousands of activists over the course of 1991. In May, the Interior Minister claimed to unearth an arms cache that Islamists had assembled as part of a plot to assassinate Ben Ali and topple the government. Although human rights organizations criticized the flimsy case that the government presented at the defendants' trials, Ben Ali invoked the plot as further justification for his war against the Islamists. From 1990–92, security forces arrested more than 8,000 individuals (Waltz 1995: 72).

Deepening Authoritarianism

By the mid-1990s, most observers agreed that the government had eliminated Ennahdha as a serious threat to Ben Ali's government. Yet the Islamist issue continued to cast a long shadow over Tunisia's politics. The crackdown on Ennahdha had decimated its organization inside Tunisia, but no one believed that it had destroyed the movement's base of support. The days of large, public marches might be over, but Ennahdha might discreetly encourage and exploit any kind of social or political protest to undermine support for the government. Into the late 1990s, the government also feared that Algeria's vicious civil war might spill over the border and spark a resurgence of Islamist support in Tunisia.

The rise of Al Qaeda globalized the government's concerns about the Islamists. In terms of its goals and the focus of its activities, Ennahdha was very much a Tunisian organization. It sought to shape the domestic political process. It might have received financial assistance and other forms of support from outside the country, but it did not participate in a transnational movement pursuing a set of global goals. In the early years of the twenty-first century, however, officials across the Maghreb and beyond became concerned that countries in North Africa and the trans-Saharan Sahel (Mali, Niger, Chad) could become fertile ground for militant organizations affiliated with Al Qaeda's effort to drive Western powers out of the Middle East, North Africa, and southwest Asia. The global nature of this movement made it much more daunting challenge. Unlike Ennahdha, most of its resources would be outside of Tunisia and beyond the government's reach. Even if militants did not try to topple Ben Ali's government directly, attacks against tourists or other Western targets in Tunisia could devastate the economy and undermine confidence in the government.

These fears were not entirely unfounded. In 1998, an organization called the Salafist Group for Preaching and Combat (GSPC) broke off from the Armed Islamic Group, the primary armed Islamist organization in Algeria. Over the next several years, the GPSC became the most important Islamist militant group in the Maghreb and the Sahel. Its ties and its theatre of operations extended into Morocco, Mauritania, Spain, France, Italy, Nigeria, Chad, and Tunisia. In April 2002, the GSPC claimed responsibility for an attack on a synagogue on the island of Djerba, an important tourist destination off Tunisia's southeastern coast. The drop in tourism receipts after that single attack cut Tunisia's growth in 2002 to the lowest level in a decade (Smith 2007).

The GSPC has not been as visibly active in Tunisia as it has been in Algeria and Morocco. But there is clear evidence that that it has deepened its ties to Al Qaeda and to Tunisian militants. In September 2006, Al Qaeda officially recognized the GSPC as its affiliate in North Africa. The organization subsequently changed its name to Al Qaeda in the Islamic Maghreb. Three and half months later, Tunisia was the scene of two dramatic shootouts between police and GSPC/Al Qaeda militants. In the first case, police in the Tunis suburb of Hammam Lif detained a young, veiled woman who led them to a hideout. The second involved a well-armed group of militants, led by a former Tunisian police officer, who had slipped across the border from Algeria and established a training camp in the mountains along the border.

Twelve militants died in these gun battles; fifteen more were arrested. Evidence collected at the scenes revealed a plot to attack hotels and the US and British embassies (ibid.).[13]

Since the early 1990s, Ben Ali has exploited fears of domestic and regional Islamists to justify and sustain an authoritarianism that extends beyond suspected Islamists. This authoritarianism involves an extension of the two basic components that developed in the early years of his tenure.

The first involves continued manipulation of electoral rules in ways that create the image of gradual reform, but that keep the opposition too weak and divided to pose any real threat. After the 1989 elections, Tunisians did not vote again in legislative elections until 1994. By that point, many observers inside Tunisia and abroad believed that the government had broken Ennahdha's ability to pose a serious threat. Nevertheless, the repression continued. Widespread accusations about human rights abuses and about the government's crackdown on all forms of opposition began to tarnish Ben Ali's image at home and abroad. Human rights organizations and the European press had begun to publicize credible reports of the government's harsh measures.

Hoping to keep the secular opposition parties engaged with him, Ben Ali agreed to modify the rules governing the 1994 elections in a way that injected a degree of the proportionality they demanded. Under the new rules, 19 of the 163 seats in the Chamber of Deputies would be set aside for opposition parties. These seats would be allocated across the parties according to their percentage of the vote. In the subsequent two legislative elections, the government increased both the number of seats in the Chamber and the number designated for the opposition.[14] For the 1999 elections, the government increased the total number of seats to 182 and set aside 34 seats for proportional distribution across the opposition parties. In 2004, the total number of seats grew to 189 and the opposition quota to 37. This gave opposition parties 20 percent of the total seats in the Chamber. Eighty percent continued to be allocated according to the old majority list system. Prior to the 2009 elections, the government approved another amendment that raises the total number of seats in the Chamber to 212 and allocates 53 of them proportionally across the opposition parties. This will increase the opposition's share to 25 percent.

A 2002 referendum created a second chamber in Tunisia's National Assembly. The new Chamber of Advisors shares law-making power with the Chamber of Deputies. It contains 126 members who are elected by professional organizations, municipal councilors, members of the Chamber of Deputies, or appointed by Ben Ali. In the 2004 elections, only 305 of the 4,555 voters belonged to opposition parties (US Department of State 2006).

These reforms are very problematic for Tunisia's opposition parties. They continue the practice of determining the distribution of legislative power by executive fiat rather than by the expressed will of the voters at the ballot box. They turn parliamentary seats into gifts, bits of patronage dispensed—or taken away—by the president and the ruling party. Significantly, and many say this is an important motivation behind the reforms, this system also pits the opposition parties against each other more than it pits them against the RCD. Given the gross imbalance in power and resources between the RCD and everyone else, a unified coalition offers the opposition the only real chance to seriously challenge the RCD's dominance. The current system makes it almost impossible for this to happen because the opposition parties must compete against each other to try to get the largest share of the seats set aside for them.

The opposition parties are well aware of these problems, and it is easy to criticize them for cooperating with the system. But this system does assure them of a degree of representation that they probably do not have the strength to win on their own under more competitive rules. Boycotting only makes sense if a party has a large enough following for its non-participation to undermine the legitimacy of the vote. In their current state, boycotting elections gains Tunisia's opposition parties nothing beyond the self-satisfaction of having been faithful to democratic principles. For parties that need to demonstrate to voters that they can do what parties are supposed to do—shape policy and deliver benefits—getting into the game is vital. As one opposition party leader put it, "We have no choice [but to accept the new rules]. We have to step into the breach that the government has opened in the hopes of getting more the next time".[15]

This is the dilemma that confronts Tunisia's opposition parties. Should they play the game for the sake of being in the game, even though the rules make it hard for them to make the game truly competitive? We saw earlier how individual party interests undermined opposition cooperation in the 1989 elections. In 2006, four parties (PUP, PSL, UDU, PVP) tried to form an alliance called the *Rencontre Démocratique*. It, too, collapsed amidst accusations that some tried to use the bloc to enhance their own standing rather than to build real unity (*Réalités* 2009).

Ben Ali has also manipulated the rules regarding presidential elections. As noted earlier, Ben Ali won broad praise in 1988 for banishing the presidency for life and for pushing a constitutional amendment that set a two-term limit on the presidency and a maximum age of 70. Then, in 2002, a referendum with strong RCD support lifted both the term and age limits. As a result, Ben Ali will run for a fifth term when Tunisians go to the polls for legislative and presidential elections in October, 2009. Other candidates have been allowed to run against Ben Ali since 1999, but the restrictive rules about who may run keep the field very small. Two candidates contested Ben Ali in the 1999 elections. Ben Ali won with 98 percent of the vote. In 2004, three opposition candidates ran for the post. Ben Ali won with 94 percent of the vote. In both elections, opposition parties complained of intimidation at the polls, lack of opposition media access, failure to distribute voting cards to opposition party members, and a lack of transparency in vote counting. Some of the opposition parties have chosen to support Ben

Ali's presidential candidacy for the sake of reducing harassment of their legislative candidates.

The second component of Ben Ali's authoritarianism has involved strict controls on civil liberties, particularly freedoms of the press and expression. These issues have attracted more attention from the European press and human rights organizations than the technical details of electoral procedures. Conversations with opposition and human rights leaders frequently emphasize Ben Ali's quick and easy reliance on the police. Over the course of the 1990s, Ben Ali dramatically expanded the country's internal security apparatus (Henry 2007: 301–2). Much of this growth took place outside the Interior Ministry and other official police forces. Critics claim that Ben Ali used a slush fund, labeled the "sovereignty fund" in the budget, to build a parallel security apparatus that he ran directly out of the presidential palace.

Many Tunisians believe that Ben Ali has been much more inclined than Bourguiba to use these security forces to intimidate the press, the judiciary, and any form of potential opposition.[16] Over the past two decades, human rights groups have assembled a very thick brief against the government for a wide range of abuses: prolonged incommunicado detentions; extracting confessions through a variety of methods of torture; surveillance; phone tapping; threats against family members; job dismissals; fabricating prurient stories about personal lives in order to discredit and blackmail; passport confiscations that prevent foreign travel; physical assaults by plain-clothed officers. The assaults, particularly on journalists, lawyers, and human rights activists, actually have become more frequent in recent years.[17] Police frequently refuse to register complaints of torture and they falsify arrest dates to extend periods of detention. Because they lack autonomy from the government, the courts provide little refuge for those accused or abused by officers of the state. Political activists who get out of jail often receive conditional releases that allow the government to jail them again if they return to opposition political activity.[18] These methods of control are not new, but many feel that Ben Ali uses them more frequently and with less finesse than Bourguiba.

This intensified repression helps to explain an important shift in the nature of political opposition in Tunisia. From the late 1960s to the early 1990s, organized social protest movements like the UGTT, the student unions, and the Islamists drove opposition politics. The opposition political parties needed these movements to generate pressure on the government because they did not have large social bases of their own.

Since the early 1990s, this kind of opposition has been rare. Journalists, lawyers, and human rights activists have replaced parties and unions as the government's principal critics. In the mid-1990s, the Tunisian Human Rights League (LTDH) became the loudest mouthpiece for this criticism. Founded in 1975, the LTDH is the oldest organization of its kind in the Arab world. After the government launched its campaign to destroy Ennahdha in 1991, the LTDH became the most vocal opponent of the government's methods and its hostility to independent expression. Individual activists became the victims of various forms of harassment. In 1993, the national assembly passed a new law allowing any citizen to join any legal association. LTDH leaders knew that the government intended to use the law to flood their organization with government supporters. The LTDH stopped operation for a time in 1992. It resumed its work in 1993, but in a less confrontational manner. Faced with continued repression, a group of thirty-five activists established a new National Committee for Liberties in Tunisia (CNLT) in 1998. The CNLT continues its non-partisan work to support and coordinate efforts to expand freedom of the press and opinion.

This shift from parties and unions to human rights activists, and from traditional socio-economic demands to rights and liberties issues, reflects a pragmatic understanding of the current political landscape. Activists realize that the electoral laws make it impossible for parties to gain any real influence on policy. They also understand that the government's repression keeps the costs of collective action high and the benefits too low. Opposition activists know that they are not strong enough to replace Ben Ali at the ballot box or otherwise. Working to establish stronger protections for free expression and political competition is the next best course. These protections are the prerequisite for any kind of meaningful opposition. Focusing on them makes strategic sense. The longer-term problem is that these issues do not mobilize large numbers of supporters. They do not resonate with the majority of the population that cares primarily about material issues.

At a deeper level, the shift in opposition issues and strategies reflects an important difference between politics under Bourguiba and Ben Ali. A certain amount of social unrest was part of the political game under Bourguiba, particularly in the 1970s and 1980s. As described earlier, it was one of the tools that competing party barons manipulated as they jockeyed for influence within the PSD. It also provided Bourguiba with excuses to dispatch troublesome figures to the political wilderness. This is not true under Ben Ali. His strategy for remaining in power does not depend on the kind of competition within the party elite that gave them incentives to ally with social protest movements and that Bourguiba manipulated to keep himself at the center of the game. Since social unrest serves no useful purpose for Ben Ali, it serves no useful purpose for other elites. Without elite allies, traditional protest methods offer dim prospects for success.

In addition to human rights abuses, Ben Ali's rule has become associated with a kind of corruption that has been relatively rare in Tunisia. Tunisia under Bourguiba certainly was corrupt in the sense that the system was rife with cronyism and manipulation. But this corruption was driven by a desire for political control or advancement rather than personal enrichment. There were cliques and clans, but they grew out of common political interests. Ben Ali's rule has generated more talk about rank criminality and personal profit within his family and his wife's family. Rumors abound of family members who receive state contracts and who profit from the privatization of state-owned firms. True or not, these tales betray a perception of the government as a clutch of families, surrounded by competent technocrats, who have turned the state into a personal income source and who have used strong-arm tactics to intimidate or eliminate competitors.

All of this has made the Tunisian presidency more insulated and isolated under Ben Ali. Bourguiba certainly was an authoritarian, but his method drew in and manipulated charismatic individuals who often had reputations and clientele bases of their own. Government ministers were political personalities in their own right. That is what made them useful to Bourguiba, but keeping them under control required great skill. Ben Ali has constructed a more centralized presidency supported by ministers who lack independent reputations and power bases. As one observer described Ben Ali's presidency: "The palace at Carthage governs in solitary and the political scene sorely lacks new political men of stature, of independent personalities" (Limam 1992: 31).

It is important to add that many secular democrats have been grudgingly complicit in Ben Ali's authoritarianism. Particularly in the late 1980s and early 1990s, Ben Ali skillfully exploited their fear of the Islamists. Were they really democrats? Could they manage the economy and instill confidence in investors? Concerned about what the Islamists might do if they came to power, many secular democrats supported Ben Ali as the lesser of two evils. Abderrahmane Tlili, secretary general of the UDU in the 1990s, spoke for many secular democrats when he described his own choice:

> As a democrat, my conscience is not clear. I know that there have been human rights abuses. But look at the countries where the Islamists have come to power—Iran, Sudan—none of them are democracies. I know Ghannouchi and Mourou [Ennahdha's second in command] very well. But if they came to power, they would have my head. I can't leave that kind of situation to my children.[19]

These concerns prompted many secular democrats to take a position of "positive neutrality" regarding the regime, to make an "objective alliance" with Ben Ali that made it easier for him to crack down on Ennahdha and expand his own power (Limam 1992: 39).

Economic conditions and policy choices have also supported Ben Ali's authoritarianism. Since the late 1980s, "Tunisia has sustained the best economic performance in the MENA [Middle East and North Africa] region" (World Bank 2000: i). Less than 7 percent of the population now falls below the official poverty level. The World Bank classifies 80 percent of the population as "middle class".

Abundant rainfall and good harvests deserve part of the credit for Tunisia's economic growth in the 1990s. But the government deserves a great deal of credit for the policies that it has implemented. From the beginning of his rule, Ben Ali has remained resolutely committed to building an economy that generates growth and jobs through private investment, exports, and deep engagement with the global economy. As in many other countries, building this kind of economy has required painful reforms: privatizations of state-owned businesses, reductions in consumer subsidies, and investment codes that take away some of the job security that workers used to enjoy.

Beyond the fact that these reforms have restored Tunisia's economy to good health, Ben Ali has tried to implement them in ways that minimize the risk of broad social unrest. For example, the government's campaigns to privatize state-owned enterprises and to lift subsidies on basic consumer goods moved more slowly than international financial institutions would have liked. The government has invested considerable sums to improve state-owned firms so that they would be more attractive to private buyers and so that these buyers would not feel compelled to dismiss large numbers of workers. In some cases, retention of the current workforce has been a condition for the sale of a state-owned firm. In both the public and private sectors, the government has become the arbiter between competing interests. Government officials are deeply involved in discussions of worker dismissals, wage negotiations, and job loss compensation. The state works to split the difference between competing interests. It uses its resources to spread the costs of economic reform and to forge compromises that minimize the number of outright "losers".

Ben Ali's government also has made a concerted effort to reduce poverty and to erode regional disparities in economic development. The centerpiece of this effort has been the National Solidarity Fund. The government established the fund in 1992 as a way of drawing the general population into the business of alleviating stubborn pockets of poverty, most of them concentrated in the southern and western portions of the country. Known popularly as "26–26", the number of the post office account to which citizens are encouraged to send donations, the fund reflects what one might describe as "compassionate authoritarianism". On the one hand, 26–26 has allowed the government to provide electricity, potable water, roads, schools, and clinics to hundreds of impoverished communities. On the other hand, and particularly in the fund's early years, many businessmen complained that the government and the RCD used strong measures to entice contributions.

These policies have created a sentiment that falls short of genuine goodwill but that provides broad, tacit support for Ben Ali's government. Most Tunisians resent the naked authoritarianism and corruption that characterize Ben Ali's rule. However, they also credit him with giving Tunisia a degree of stability, efficiency, and prosperity that makes it the envy of the region. When they consider the region as a whole, they conclude that their quality of life is higher than their neighbors' and the severity of their authoritarianism is no worse. No opposition party can offer a credible alternative that would improve on the status quo, so many Tunisians have simply given up on politics.

3 Stability, reform, and development in Tunisia's economy

Small size generally is not an asset to economic development. In most respects, this certainly has been true in Tunisia's case. Along with its arid climate, Tunisia's small size endows the country with a limited resource base and small domestic markets.

In at least one sense, however, Tunisia's small size has been a boon. If the country's borders extended further east into Libya, or west toward Algeria's oil and gas fields at Hassi Messaoud, Tunisia might have developed the difficulties that have afflicted many countries "blessed" with large hydrocarbon reserves.[1] The absence of easy wealth from oil and gas has forced a steady pragmatism that has served Tunisia well.

This is not to say that economic development has been easy for Tunisia or that policymakers have always made the best choices. As in many developing countries, the government historically has been deeply involved in the economy as both policy architect and owner of strategic industries and services. By the mid-1980s, this heavy state involvement and changes in the global economy had created many of the problems that plagued other developing economies: large debts, a bloated and inefficient public sector, weak incentives for private investment. But Tunisia's economic crisis was much less severe than most, and it was able to recover much more quickly than most. That quick recovery and the impressive record that Tunisia has achieved in the past decade stem in large part from the foundation laid in the 1960s and 1970s.

The rhetoric of Tunisia's development strategy has changed a great deal over the course of its independent history. But the substance has changed much less. Some basic "givens" account for this consistency. Tunisia's small size and limited resource base, its proximity to Europe, and its economic ties to France give it relatively few options. Tunisia simply does not have the resources to experiment with a wide variety of development strategies. If this has freed Tunisia from protracted battles and difficult choices about the basic nature of its development strategy, it has also created another fundamental challenge. Given these constraints, how can the government make essentially the same development strategy work in changing economic and political circumstances?

Leadership has been critical. As the following section describes, regional and domestic political considerations prompted Bourguiba to adopt some of the socialist rhetoric that was popular across the region in the 1960s. But he set careful limits on "Tunisian socialism". Since the late 1980s, Ben Ali has prudently managed Tunisia's economy by making choices that encourage private investment and export-driven growth while avoiding the social and political risks of excessive neo-liberalism. Both presidents' ability to navigate a pragmatic course between ideological extremes has helped to make Tunisia the region's economic success story. But daunting challenges remain. Tunisia's deeper integration into the regional economy will test the government's ability to pursue growth while maintaining social stability and political control.

From the Market to "Tunisian Socialism"

Habib Bourguiba stepped into independence with two central goals: to consolidate power and to lay the foundations for economic growth. These goals were intimately related. From the beginning of his career, Bourguiba's case to the Tunisian people relied heavily on economic issues. He emphasized independence as both a matter of principle and as a prerequisite to any meaningful improvement in working and living conditions for average Tunisians. He argued that nationalists should support him rather than Ben Youssef because he would reduce the power of traditional elites and distribute wealth and opportunities more broadly. The Neo-Destour had built much of its popular support by functioning as an effective patron–client network that provided vital goods and services to its members. Now that independence had been won, and with unemployment at nearly 30 percent, Bourguiba felt strong pressure to produce jobs and growth quickly. Additionally, in his struggle for control of the Neo-Destour, Bourguiba curried the UGTT's favor by supporting its socialist development strategy in 1955.

But Bourguiba was no socialist and neither were most members of the Neo-Destour. Merchants, landowners, and entrepreneurs constituted influential constituencies within the party. They had bankrolled the Neo-Destour since its birth and Bourguiba knew that they were vital to the country's economic future. Nationalizing farms and businesses and imposing centralized economic planning might spark capital flight. It might also prompt wealthy Tunisians to throw their support behind Ben Youssef's more conservative wing of the party.

Bourguiba was also concerned about the French. He had long argued that Tunisia's economic development depended on strong relations with its former colonial power. At independence, French interests still held all of Tunisia's iron, zinc, sea salt, and lead deposits. They controlled most of the phosphates, at least 400,000 hectares of the best agricultural land, and 55 percent of all bank capital (Ben Romdhane 1985: 262). Bourguiba rejected the idea of an Algerian-style uprising against France in part because he wanted to sustain French economic assistance. Throughout the protracted negotiations leading to independence, he pledged that his government would respect French property rights in Tunisia. When France reduced its aid to Tunisia in 1957 because of Tunisian support for Algerian independence, the US quickly stepped into its place as the country's primary aid provider. US aid totaled $239.2 million between 1956–61—a sum equal to 47 percent of Tunisia's gross total investment for the period (Ben Romdhane 1985: 263). This aid came with strong encouragement to pursue a liberal economic development strategy (Toumi 1989: 54).

Once the Youssefist threat to his leadership had subsided, encouraging French and American assistance and keeping the support of Tunisian capital became two of Bourguiba's top priorities. He also needed to ensure that the UGTT did not dictate economic policy. Consequently, Bourguiba moved away from the centrally planned economy that the trade union advocated. He opted instead for a form of state capitalism that encouraged and directed the growth of the private sector. In the late 1950s, the Tunisian government nationalized public transport and the ports, as well as water, gas, and electricity services. It began buying portions of the phosphate sector and established a central bank and three development banks. Through these institutions, the government provided investment capital, tax holidays, and protective tariffs that officials hoped would encourage private sector growth.

They did not. Despite these measures, the Tunisian economy deteriorated steadily over the first five years of independence. Investments fell by 50 percent between 1956–61. Equipment imports plummeted.[2] Development funds remained underutilized and job creation lagged. By 1958, capital flight to France totaled $70,000,000. The lack of investment in productive sectors forced the government to borrow heavily from abroad in order to fund housing, communications, transports, and electrification projects. The general price index rose 16 percent between 1956–61 while wages remained at 1955 levels (Ben Romdhane 1985: 260; Grissa 1991: 109–10; Moore 1965: 195; Poncet 1970: 94; Toumi 1989: 54).

Why did Tunisia's private sector not respond to the government's incentives? Most scholars agree that it had little to do with Bourguiba's government. The failure to invest did not constitute a "no confidence" vote. Rather, the lack of productive investment was a function of the risk-averse nature of Tunisia's private sector. Of the few entrepreneurs with substantial capital, many chose to buy French firms rather than start new ones (Bellin 1991: 48). On the whole, however, Tunisia's private sector was made up of small, family-owned enterprises. Even if they had the capital to invest in growth, they lacked the technical and managerial skills necessary to run larger operations (Grissa 1991: 109–10). Business owners had little experience with banks, saving, obtaining credit, or investing for the long term. They were accustomed to operating on a day-to-day basis, not investing in long-term growth. If they chose to invest at all, they chose speculative opportunities that offered quick returns, not productive investments that would create growth and jobs but that also involved greater risk and deferred profits. Faced with a private sector that could not provide the engine for long-term economic growth, and fearful that rising debt and unemployment would make Tunisia fertile ground for the more radical pan-Arab movements gaining popularity across the region in the late 1950s, Bourguiba decided that the state would have to step into the breach.[3]

Tunisia's "Socialist Experiment"

In 1961, Bourguiba announced a dramatic shift in Tunisia's economic development strategy. The chief architect of this new strategy was Ahmed Ben Salah, the former secretary-general of the UGTT and the author of the union's socialist economic development plan in 1955–56. Rehabilitated since his removal as head of the UGTT, Ben Salah's position as the Minister of Plan and National Economy gave him the opportunity to implement the policies that Bourguiba had rejected at independence.

These policies began with a planned economy. In Ben Salah's view, one shared widely in development circles in the 1950s and 1960s, only the government possessed the resources and the global, long-term view required for national development. Only the government could rise above the risk-averse, day-to-day survival concerns of small business owners and see how various sectors of the economy needed to work together in the service of long-term development. This global view allowed the state to direct investments to vital sectors, to provide the necessary infrastructure, and to construct the linkages between sectors that would pursue a single, coherent set of development goals.

Industrialization figured at the top of those goals. As long as Tunisia had to buy expensive manufactured products from France and other industrialized countries, and as long as Tunisia had only cheap agricultural goods to sell abroad, the country would remain trapped in a perpetual cycle of underdevelopment. The difference in prices and demand for manufactured and primary goods meant that Tunisia and other developing countries would always pay more for manufactured imports than they earned through their exports. In this way, the international division of labor between industrialized and non-industrialized countries would allow the former to become progressively wealthier while the latter became progressively poorer. The only way out of this cycle was to industrialize, to produce at home some of the goods that otherwise would have to be imported. In time, developing countries might also be able to sell more of their manufactured goods abroad. But the initial goal was to produce manufactured goods that could substitute for expensive imports. This effort to industrialize developing economies came to be known as import-substituting industrialization, or ISI.[4]

Individual ISI strategies reflected differences in countries' economic endowments and political dynamics. Oil-rich countries like Algeria could rely on oil and gas sales for funds that they could invest in industrialization.[5] Countries lacking this easy source of investment capital had to look for it elsewhere. Most governments borrowed from abroad. In Tunisia, the agricultural sector also played a vital role. A fundamental part of Ben Salah's development strategy involved the creation of cooperatives that would reform and modernize the agricultural sector. Across much of the country-side, farm holdings were too small and the families too poor to invest in modern techniques that would boost production. The use of modern fertilizers, combines, irrigation systems, and other large equipment did not make economic sense on small plots. Cooperatives would unify small holdings into units that were large enough to use modern techniques and equipment. They also would benefit from a professional staff. The result would be an agricultural sector that contributed to the development effort by serving as the primary source of internal capital accumulation. The quality of rural life would improve, eroding regional disparities and fostering a more robust national identity.

The social consequences that would follow from these changes were as important to Ben Salah as the economic ones. "Tunisian socialism" was never about an abstract political and economic philosophy. Bourguiba emphasized repeatedly that socialism in Tunisia was a very specific thing that had nothing to do with class conflict, Marxism, communism, or revolution. It was about planning and using the resources and structures of the state to build a more independent economy and a stronger sense of national solidarity. He tried to ground it in Islam by describing the companions of the prophet as socialists in the sense that they acted as members of one family. The whole strategy—the increased focus on education, the cooperatives, the state-owned enterprises—was intended to liberate individual Tunisians from "archaic" social values and break down exploitative social relations. In so doing, this humanistic form of socialist development would create a new Tunisian society that was both more modern and more unified.

The rhetoric surrounding Ben Salah's plan certainly made it sound like a fundamental change in the government's development philosophy. "Planned economies", "cooperatives", and the repeated use of the term "socialism" all suggested a new and very different orientation. By all accounts, that honestly is what Ben Salah intended. But not Bourguiba. He was no more a socialist in 1961 than he had been in 1956. What had changed was the political and economic environment. In the 1950s and 1960s, secular, left-leaning pan-Arabism was the most powerful political force in the Middle East and North Africa. Across the region, nationalist movements and newly-independent governments called for the unification of Arab governments and for "socialist" development strategies that could produce economic independence and distribute wealth more broadly.

By 1961 it was clear that Algeria soon would become an independent country guided by an explicitly socialist development philosophy. As Tunisia's economy deteriorated in the late 1950s, Bourguiba feared that he would become vulnerable to rising discontent. That discontent would likely express itself in the language of the secular left. It might also receive support from others in the region, particularly Egypt's President Gamal Abd al-Nasser, who championed pan-Arabism as a means of enhancing their own power. By tacking to the left in 1961, Bourguiba hoped to protect himself from these political challenges.

In reality, Tunisia's "socialist experiment" did not mark a fundamental break with the past. The state did take a more active role in industrializing the economy and improving infrastructure. But Bourguiba carefully crafted the strategy in ways that protected what one analyst called his "implicit contract" with private capital (Ben Romdhane 1995: 273–4). For example, in creating the roughly 1,500 cooperatives established between 1961 and 1969, the government carefully avoided sectors with large numbers of influential Tunisian landowners and business owners. Despite the government's emphasis on agricultural reform, it established only 700 cooperatives in the agricultural sector. These cooperatives did not take in holdings larger than 40 hectares, so they never touched large, politically influential olive growers in the Sahel region. Bourguiba even ordered officials at the Central Bank to control the amount of money that the banks made available for Ben Salah's program (Moore, 1991: 68–9).

In sharp contrast to Algeria and other countries where industrializing governments adopted policies more hostile to private business interests, the Tunisian government actively encouraged the private sector. It wanted private businesses to grow and make profits. To that end, it continued to provide tax holidays, protected markets, guaranteed loans, and subsidized credit. But it wanted the private sector to make its profits through productive, job-creating activities rather than through speculation (Bellin 1991: 50). Over the course of the "socialist sixties", state credits and assistance to the private sector accounted for 75 percent of total investment (Toumi 1989: 63). Additionally, most landowners and business owners continued to use family contacts and other personal ties to the party and state bureaucracies to protect their interests. Thus, through a wide range of protections and exemptions, Tunisia's socialism actively supported the growth of the country's nascent bourgeoisie. Local private investment rose an average of 6.6 million dinars each year between 1962–69. Most of this investment gravitated toward sectors that benefited from the state's investment in infrastructure, but remained free of its control: tourism, hotels, textiles, construction (Ben Romdhane 1985: 270).

Even critics concede that Tunisia's economic policies in the 1960s generated important long-term benefits for the country. Between 1962 and 1969, the government invested 90 million dinars a year in a broad range of social and economic projects. Expenditures for education, roads, water, electricity, and health care increased dramatically. The percentage of the population living below the poverty level fell from 70–75 percent in the early 1960s to 40–45 percent at the end of the decade (Azaiez 1980: 397–9;

Kleve and Stolper 1974: 9, 14–15). The number of state-owned enterprises grew from 25 in 1960 to nearly 185 in 1970 (Grissa 1991: 111). These firms—including the SOGITEX textile plant in Ksar Hellal, the National Cellulose Company in Kasserine, the oil refinery at Bizerte, the heavy industrial furnace at Menzel-Bourguiba, and the National Sugar Company in Beja—laid the foundations for a modern, industrialized economy in Tunisia. Private investment increased, as well. Private investments in manufacturing and tourism grew from less than one million dinars in 1962 to more than twenty million in 1970 (Ben Romdhane 1985: 271).

Beneath these accomplishments, however, the policies of the 1960s also created serious economic and social disturbances. The agricultural cooperatives, the touchstone of Ben Salah's plan, failed miserably. Small farmers resisted the collectivization program, and government authorities frequently used harsh measures to enforce it. The policy converted farmers into hourly employees of the state. But because the cooperatives frequently incorporated more workers than the land could support, and because the government encouraged mechanization, many farmers remained underemployed.[6] Their incomes dropped dramatically. Additionally, depriving farmers of ownership and severing the connection between their work and their incomes eroded incentives to produce the surplus that the state needed. These inefficiencies and disincentives, combined with inept decisions by bureaucrats who knew too little about farming in the particular regions they managed, took a heavy toll on Tunisia's agricultural production. The agricultural sector's portion of Tunisia's GDP fell from 24.2 percent to 16.5 percent over the course of the 1960s. The value of agricultural production fell from 102,500 dinars in 1965 to 63,800 dinars in 1967 (J. Zouari 1993: 8).

Declining agricultural production cost the government dearly in two ways. Because the cooperatives rarely generated a surplus, the government had to borrow heavily to fund the central pillar of its economic strategy. Additionally, the country that once was the breadbasket of Rome began to import food. While agricultural production fell over the course of the 1960s, the Tunisian population grew by some 800,000. Feeding that population forced the Tunisian government to begin buying wheat abroad. Those imports, combined with heavy borrowing to fund the cooperatives and new social and industrial projects, quadrupled Tunisia's debt over the course of the 1960s. The trade deficit rose 50 percent in 1968–69 alone. Debt service consumed 42 percent of exports. The September 13, 1969 issue of *The Economist* noted that Tunisia "receives more foreign aid per person . . . than about any other country in the world". As they did across much of the developing world, policies intended to make Tunisia economically independent rendered the country more dependent on foreign assistance than ever before.

The industrial sector did not fare much better. One study found that Tunisia's mining and manufacturing enterprises generated profits only one year between 1963 and 1969 (Kleve and Stolper 1974: 23). Moreover, and despite the proliferation of new enterprises, unemployment remained above 20 percent. Those who did find jobs in these plants did not see their material conditions improve dramatically. The emphasis on investment for future growth also meant an emphasis on austerity. Although the government gave small pay raises to workers at the bottom of the pay scale in December 1965, the real minimum wage rose by a feeble 3 percent between 1962 and 1969. The real average wage rose by only 1 percent. During this same period, the cost of living rose 30 percent (A. Zouari 1990: 442–3).

By the end of the 1960s, the government's tightening authoritarianism could no longer prevent outbursts of popular discontent. In 1968–69, peasant protests against the cooperative program turned violent in Ouardanine, Msaken, and Ksar Hellal. Railroad workers, dockworkers, and phosphate miners launched wildcat strikes. On university campuses, groups affiliated with the Tunisian Communist Party and organizations further to the left organized student protests. They argued that Ben Salah's socialism was too timid. Tunisia's economic and social difficulties stemmed from the fact that the government had failed to break the exploitative power of private interests and had erected an abusive state bureaucracy.

Tunisia's economic and social deterioration played into the hands of Ben Salah's many critics inside the government. Socialism never generated much heartfelt enthusiasm inside a government and ruling party that contained strong private sector interests. The fact that the ruling party changed its name to the Destourian Socialist Party (PSD) in 1964 had more to do with authoritarianism than conviction. It is also fair to suggest that some of the hostility was personal. As noted earlier, many party leaders saw Ben Salah as an arrogant upstart who trafficked in an imported ideology for his own political gain. They resented his rapid rise and his concentration of power.

For his part, Ben Salah countered that the cooperative program was in trouble because it was not big enough. It had failed because it did not take in the large, prosperous farms in the north and in the Sahel. To succeed, the program had to cover the entire agricultural economy. When Ben Salah announced new policies that would do just that in early 1969, intense opposition from the private sector and fear that Ben Salah was becoming too powerful prompted Bourguiba to sack and jail him. Ben Salah escaped prison and fled the country in 1973.

Infitah

In 1970, Bourguiba steered Tunisia's economy—or at least official rhetoric about the economy—back toward the market. To direct this effort, he appointed Hedi Nouira to serve as prime minister. Nouira was a vocal advocate of a more liberal economic strategy. He had always opposed Ben Salah's socialism and he spent the 1960s at the head of Tunisia's Central Bank. Bourguiba put him there, in part, because he wanted Nouira to control the amount of money that the banks made available to Ben Salah.

Under Nouira's leadership, Tunisia became the first country in the Middle East and North Africa to implement the kinds of liberalizing reforms that came to be known across the region as *infitah*, Arabic for "opening".[7] A long-time student of European political economy, Nouira believed that Tunisia had no choice but to pursue an export-oriented development strategy. As a small, resource-poor, and predominantly agricultural country, Tunisia would always have to import a wide range of manufactured goods. To pay for these imports, create jobs, and reduce its debt, Tunisia had to expand exports of the small number of commodities for which it enjoyed a comparative advantage on regional markets—phosphates, petroleum, olive oil, and textiles. The government also had to reduce its expenditures and attract more domestic and foreign investment. Nouira summed up his philosophy thus: "In place of an administered economy, it is necessary to construct an economy obeying the rules of efficiency and profitability. The law of the market is hard, but it is the law of truth and of progress" (Ben Romdhane 1985: 275).

In an effort to attract new private investment, the government created an *Agence de Promotion des Investissements*. The new office helped to stream-line investment procedures and pre-established some industrial zones in locations that already had adequate infrastructure (Findlay 1984: 228). The real boost, however, came from two new investment laws. In 1972 the government passed Law 72-38, a measure aimed primarily at attracting new foreign capital into export-oriented sectors. The law exempted firms producing for export from corporate income tax for ten years. The firms then would enjoy a reduced tax rate for ten more years. The law also exempted firms from customs duties on imported materials needed to pro-duce the goods that they then exported. Firms producing for the local market benefited from tax breaks on reinvested profits and exemptions from customs duties and turnover taxes on imported inputs. Two years later, Law 74-74 expanded these incentives to attract Tunisian private investment and linked the incentives to the number of jobs created as well as to the amount of money invested. New firms also benefited from improved credit facilities, low property rents, and freedom to repatriate profits (ibid.: 228).

As important as these reforms were, it is important to emphasize that they did not constitute a drastic change from an economy managed by the state to one managed by the market. While Nouira believed firmly in the economic benefits of markets, he also believed that the state must play a powerful role. Between 1973 and 1984, the government built 110 new state-owned enterprises (Grissa 1991: 112). It also dedicated considerable resources to consumer subsidies and to a wide range of investments in social programs, wages, and infrastructure. State policy, not market forces, dictated interest rates, monetary policy, the allocation of public and private investment, and access to credit.

Infitah did not change the state's relationship to the economy as much it changed how it talked about the economy. As Chedly Ayari, one of Tunisia's leading economists and economic policymakers describes it, Bourguiba and Nouira wanted, "to restore confidence in the private sector, to give it a taste for enterprise, initiative and risk" (Ben Mansour 1993: 16). But it was always clear that this would happen under close state supervision and direction. Although he extolled the virtues of the market, Nouira remained "a man of the state, a man for whom a powerful, strong and uncontested state should prevail" (ibid.: 16).

The government's new measures produced many of their desired results. The state continued to dominate strategic sectors like phosphates, electricity, water, hydrocarbons, petro-chemicals, and transport. But private investors because major players in tourism, textiles, and light manufacturing. Investment in Tunisia also benefited from economic stagnation in Europe. Low growth rates there drove surplus capital "toward developing countries where higher rates of return could be obtained" (Pfeifer 1996: 2). Between 1973–78, more than 500 foreign firms established factories in Tunisia and invested approximately 57 million dinars. By 1978, private investment in light manufacturing industries had climbed to 14 million dinars. In 1973–78, these investments created over 86,000 new industrial and manufacturing jobs (Findlay 1984: 228).

In addition to the growth in private investment, good weather boosted production for cereals and olives. Olive oil production rose from an annual average of 40,000 tons in the late 1960s to an average of 114,250 tons between 1971 and 1974. Prices for that oil rose from 35 dinars per ton in 1971 to 771 dinars per ton in 1974. In all, the value of Tunisia's olive oil exports rose from 8.7 million dinars in 1971 to an average of 48 million dinars per year between 1972 and 1974.

Other export commodities fared equally well. In addition to the well-known rise in oil prices in the early 1970s, phosphate prices climbed from just under 4.2 dinars per ton in 1972 to 17.9 dinars in 1974. In all, the value of Tunisia's exports quadrupled in 1970–74, rising from 98.8 million dinars in to nearly 398 million dinars. This combination of favorable economic trends generated annual growth rates of 8–10 percent and placed Tunisia among the top ten countries in terms of GDP growth per person (Ben Romdhane 1985: 277–9).

From the government's perspective, this growth also generated important political benefits. Since the late 1960s, the most critical opposition had come from the left. More specifically, it came from activists affiliated with the outlawed Communist Party and from other leftist organizations. As described in the previous chapter, these activists made a concerted effort to turn student organizations and the labor movement into battering rams against the government. Economic growth provided the government with a critical weapon for battling this threat. It allowed the state, through a new wage bargaining system, to provide substantial pay increases to workers. The government negotiated these raises directly with the union for workers in the public sector. It pressed the employers' organization to do likewise for workers in the private sector.

Unfortunately, the pillars of this prosperity began to crumble in the mid-1970s. After 1975, increasing regional competition cut into the prices for Tunisian olive oil and phosphates and eroded Tunisia's share of those markets. Olive oil prices slipped from 771 dinars per ton in 1974 to 517 dinars in 1977. Tunisia harvested 265,000 tons of olives in the 1976–77 season, but it exported only 78,000 tons. In addition to reducing Tunisia's export earnings, the inability to export more of the harvest created a costly storage problem. Phosphate prices tumbled from 23.3 dinars per ton in 1975 to 10.6 dinars in 1977. Phosphate exports fell from 47 million dinars in 1974–75 to 22 million in 1977. The onset of a recession in Europe prompted many governments to close their borders to Tunisian exports, including textiles. The total value of Tunisia's exports dropped from 387.7 million dinars in 1974 to 344.3 million dinars in 1977. At the same time, increased food and consumer goods imports generated a serious trade imbalance. External borrowing pushed Tunisia's debt from 100 million dinars in 1974 to 294 million dinars in 1977 (Ben Romdhane 1985: 280–1).

This economic downturn took a heavy toll on jobs and incomes. Falling exports forced many private sector plants to close. The new European tariffs forced nineteen textile plants out of business in 1978 alone, eliminating 2,000 jobs (Findlay 1984: 229).[8] Unemployment rose across the economy and both the government and private owners became less willing to increase wages. That did not sit well with workers struggling to keep up with inflation rates that had climbed to 10 percent by 1975. These pressures contributed to the rising tide of worker unrest that culminated in the January 1978 general strike.

Tunisia's economy continued to deteriorate through the 1980s. A combination of domestic and regional factors accounted for the deepening crisis. At home, the new private investment into light manufacturing industries in the mid-1970s did not boost output as dramatically as many hoped. The more capital-intensive sectors that continued to rely on state investment (metal and chemical industries) performed better. As a result, Tunisia's Fifth Development Plan (1977–81) placed renewed emphasis on state investment (Findlay 1984: 230). By 1984, Tunisia had built 295 public enterprises. In many of these plants, the government invested in capital-intensive technology that reduced the number of needed workers. At the same time, however, the government felt intense pressure to provide new jobs to the growing working-age population. Political concerns carried the day and government-owned firms hired more workers than they actually needed. By the early 1980s, the public enterprise sector was overstaffed by 20 percent (Saghir 1993: 7). Many public enterprises operated at only 40–60 percent of their capacity because of overstaffing and low productivity. To keep them afloat, government transfers to these plants rose from 8 percent of government spending in 1972 to 17.5 percent in 1984. This willingness to subsidize public enterprises made the problem worse by taking away any incentives to become more efficient (Grissa 1991: 112). In total, government investment in Tunisia's state enterprises had climbed from 12 million dinars in 1969 to nearly 200 million in 1980 (Vandewalle 1992: 115).

Food subsidies constituted another substantial drain on the state budget. In 1980, the *Caisse Générale de Compensation*, the agency that manages consumer subsidies, ran a deficit in excess of 100 million dinars. Poor harvests in the 1980s continued to drive up the costs of a subsidy program that many believed encouraged consumer waste, discouraged agricultural production, and benefited middle and upper income households more than poor families. In 1987, the Caisse spent 220 million dinars on subsidies for wheat, flour, milk, sugar, cooking oil, and other basic goods (Harik 1992: 212).

Together, subsidies for food and inefficient public enterprises boosted government spending and budget deficits. Those deficits, in turn, forced the government to borrow money abroad. Ironically, Tunisia's economic success in the 1970s worked to its disadvantage when the government needed to borrow in the 1980s. Because Tunisia had established such a good reputation with international financial institutions, it could not borrow at concessional rates. By 1983, commercial borrowing to cover rising budget deficits pushed Tunisia's debt to 45 percent of GNP. By 1987, debt had risen to 74 percent of GDP. Servicing that debt consumed 29 percent of Tunisia's export earnings (Grissa 1991: 112–13; Pfeifer 1996: 45–6). Real salaries fell 30 percent between 1983 and 1988 while inflation climbed 10 percent each year (Ben Romdhane 1990: 175).

Regional economic developments made it more difficult for Tunisia to dig its way out of the deepening debt crisis. Recession and rising protectionism in Europe reduced demand for Tunisian exports. Rising interest rates made it more difficult for debtor countries to service their debt. The stream of surplus capital that flowed into Tunisia when European economies stagnated in the 1970s reversed in the early 1980s (Pfeifer 1996: 25).

Structural Economic Reform

By 1986, Tunisia's mounting debt and its overvalued currency had created a serious foreign exchange crisis. At its most extreme point, the Central Bank had enough foreign exchange to cover only one week's worth of imports. To halt the slide toward bankruptcy, the government decided to reschedule its debt, to seek assistance in covering its balance of payments shortage from the International Monetary Fund (IMF), and to negotiate a structural adjustment agreement with the IMF and the World Bank.

After Ben Ali came to power in November, 1987, implementing these reforms in a way that maintained political stability became one of his government's top priorities. Like most structural adjustment programs, Tunisia's sought to accomplish two fundamental goals: to reduce and rationalize government expenditures and to boost private investment in an economy that generates growth and jobs through exports. The government has pursued these goals through a careful sequence of mutually-reinforcing measures that reduce government spending, steadily replace government control with market forces, and that integrate Tunisia more deeply into the global economy.

Some of the earliest and most important reforms focused on exchange rates and the banking and finance sector. The government devalued the currency to help make Tunisian exports more attractive. It raised interest rates and then deregulated them. This move, along with measures that introduced competition between banks and gave them more freedom to make credit and lending decisions, allocated financial resources more efficiently and created stronger incentives for savings and investment. By 1997, over 90 percent of the credits from Tunisian financial institutions went to the private sector (Dillman 1998: 16).

To encourage private investment, the government issued a new investment code in 1989 that provided tax breaks and lower customs fees to investors in export-oriented activities. The government modified the code in 1993 to add new incentives for foreign investment in areas such as automobile assembly, agro-business, and oil exploration. Additional measures improved the business environment by reducing administrative red tape and making the enforcement of regulations more uniform and transparent.

All of these measures were intended to make it easier for export-oriented businesses to obtain bank credit and attract private investors. Other measures sought to reduce the government's own spending. Over the course of the early 1990s, the government progressively reduced consumer subsidies and targeted them more carefully on a handful of basic food items that are consumed predominantly by the poor. The government also began to privatize some of the state-owned enterprises that consumed so much money in the 1970s and 1980s.

The government's approach to privatization illustrates its commitment to implementing structural reform in a way that minimizes the risk of political unrest. While Western governments and financial institutions have lauded Tunisia as one of the most successful implementers of market-oriented reforms, they have expressed frustration at times over the slow pace of privatization. That slowness has been intentional. Across the region, young unemployed men have provided a fertile demographic for Islamist movements. Thus, preserving jobs and creating new ones has been more than an economic goal for Ben Ali's government. It is a primary component in the effort to combat social unrest generally and Islamism in particular. The government's approach to privatization reflects this political goal.

While Tunisia took some small steps toward privatization as early as 1986, the government did not launch a concerted privatization program until 1989. The first phase of the privatization campaign, which ran through 1994, targeted small enterprises in the service (tourism, commerce) and agribusiness sectors that were struggling financially and that cost the government money. The government sold most of these firms, many of which were hotels, directly to private buyers with stipulations that restricted the new owners' ability to reduce the workforce. Because of these restrictions, and because many of these firms had struggled to pay salaries regularly, workers often welcomed these privatizations. This first wave privatized approximately 45 firms whose total worth was estimated at $90 million (Pangaea Partners 1997: 1).[9]

The second phase of the government's privatization program began in 1994 and expanded to take in larger and more profitable firms. By extending the program's scope in this way, the government demonstrated that it did not see privatization simply as a way to cut costs by getting rid of unproductive firms. It signaled a clear commitment to private ownership as a more efficient and dynamic method of generating growth and jobs. This second phase of privatizations also coincided with reforms that modernized the stock exchange by separating its operating and regulatory operations and by converting it into a private enterprise owned by registered brokers. While the first privatizations involved direct sales to new owners, the second wave included sales of blocks of shares or public offers on the stock market.

Since the late 1990s, the government has steadily increased the number, the size, and the prominence of the firms it is willing to privatize. It has even begun to privatize firms in previously untouchable "strategic" sectors like transportation, communications, and banking. In one of the more recent and dramatic actions, the government sold off 35 percent of Tunisie Telecom in 2006. By Spring 2009, according to the Tunisian government, 217 enterprises had been privatized or restructured (Prime Ministry of the Republic of Tunisia 2009). Just over half of these cases involved total privatizations, the other half involved partial privatizations, concessions, liquidations, or public offerings of capital. The government has used proceeds from these sales to, among other things, pay down the country's debt.

By the mid-1990s, these reforms—bolstered by good harvests, healthy tourism receipts, and wise public investment—had restored consistent economic growth. Tunisia's GDP grew at an annual average rate of 3.9 percent from 1985–95. Per capita GNP grew at an annual rate of 1.7 percent. The sources of this growth became more diverse as manufactured goods, hydrocarbons, and services made up a larger percentage of GDP. At the same time, inflation fell to 4.5 percent. From 1987–92, private sector investment rose to 51 percent of total investment (Dillman 1998: 16). By 1997, foreign investment exceeded $500 million. The current account deficit dropped from 8.5 percent of GDP in 1981–86 to 3.9 percent in 1987–92. The budget deficit fell from 3.9 percent of GDP in 1989 to 2.3 percent in 1993. While Tunisia's total debt increased from $4.9 billion in 1985 to $8.5 billion in 1992, debt as percentage of GNP fell from 71 percent to 56 percent. The debt service ratio fell from 25 percent to 20 percent. By 1996, the ratio was down to 17 percent (ibid.: 12).

Tunisia and the European Economy

One of the most important components of the government's reform plan concerns Tunisia's ties to the global economy in general and to Europe in particular. Tunisia's government has pursued growth through exports since the early 1970s.[10] Under Ben Ali, however, the government has been much more willing to integrate itself more thoroughly into the regional economy and to open the economy to imports. Tunisia joined the World Trade Organization in 1990 and freed 85 percent of its imports from quantitative restrictions as early as 1992. In 1993, Ben Ali established a new Ministry of International Cooperation and Foreign Investment. Exports grew at an annual rate of 7.1 percent from 1985–95, and Tunisia's export profile became more diverse as textiles, mechanical, and electrical products accounted for a larger portion of total exports.

By far the most important step into the global economy came in July 1995, when Tunisia became the first country on the southern shore of the Mediterranean to sign an association agreement with the European Union. The accord established a 12-year transition period that would culminate in a free trade zone for industrial goods between Tunisia and the European Union.[11] Along with its other reforms, Tunisia began dismantling import tariffs in 1996 as part of the transition to free trade with the EU.

Joining a free trade zone with Europe would create significant new opportunities for Tunisia. It would facilitate European tourism, a vital source of foreign exchange earnings. More importantly, it would give Tunisian products access to a market of some 500 million consumers. This would open a vast new frontier for existing firms, but it also would attract new foreign investment. Tunisia already offered tax incentives and subsidies to export-oriented businesses. But EU protectionism made it difficult for Tunisian-made products to enter European economies. Without that access, Tunisia's own market was too small to make it an attractive location for new job-creating and export-earning businesses. The free trade zone would change all of that. It would make Tunisia an attractive jumping off place for companies interested in gaining access to European markets. By coming to Tunisia, companies would benefit from tax incentives; close proximity to European, African, and Middle Eastern markets; lower wages than in Europe; well-developed infrastructure for transportation, electricity, water, and gas; and an educated workforce. This would be a powerful combination of assets for a country seeking to attract high-tech manufacturing and service sector investments.

If free trade would create new opportunities, it also would generate substantial competitive pressure. The same freedom that would give Tunisia access to other markets would give other countries greater access to Tunisia's. Tunisian firms that could not compete in terms of price and quality would lose their home markets. The textile industry became a particular point of concern in this regard. Textile manufacturing had grown in Tunisia under the protection of a global multi-fiber agreement that allowed developing countries to impose quotas on imported textiles. These quotas shielded Tunisian-made goods from competition with less expensive goods produced in lower-wage countries. As part of the Uruguay Round of global trade negotiations, the World Trade Organization agreed to phase out these quotas by 2005. The end of these import restrictions would expose Tunisian textile manufacturers to keener competition at home and abroad. The stakes would be high for the entire economy since textiles represent 40 percent of Tunisia's exports and over half of all manufacturing jobs.

To prepare for the challenges created by freer trade, the Tunisian government, with the support of the European Union, established a ten-year program in 1996 to help Tunisian firms become more competitive. Labeled the *mise à niveau*, or "upgrading", program, the new initiative provided grants that paid for 20 percent of the value of capital investments that would enhance quality and efficiency. It placed particular emphasis on the small and medium-sized plants that make up 80 percent of Tunisia's manufacturing sector.[12]

In addition to this support from the EU, Tunisia also benefited from the strong support of international financial institutions. Tunisia was able to negotiate a $125 million standby agreement with the IMF for the November, 1986–May 1988 period. That agreement was followed in July, 1988 by a three-year extended fund facility that was extended for one year in 1991 (Dillman 1998: 9). Tunisia continued to borrow heavily through the early 1990s. As early as 1987, Tunisia had contracted $300 million in new World Bank loans. By 2005, the country's foreign debt had climbed to $19.2 million. This is a large figure compared to many comparable countries, but most of these loans came from multilateral and bilateral sources. This allowed Tunisia to enjoy lower interest rates and longer terms of maturity than it would have received from commercial lenders (ibid.: 12). These loans, along with debt rescheduling, allowed the government to continue making productive investments that helped to restore growth quickly and to maintain political stability through a reform process that generated serious economic and political tensions in most of Tunisia's neighbors.

The period from January, 2005–January, 2008 was critical for Tunisia. The first date marked the end of the multi-fiber protections for Tunisian textiles; the second marked the beginning of the industrial free trade zone with Europe. At this point, Tunisia seems to have managed these transitions well. Annual growth averaged 4.5 percent from 2002–6. It rose to 6.3 percent in 2007—the highest level in a decade—thanks to strong European demand for Tunisian products and healthy performances in the service, agricultural, and manufacturing sectors. Textiles weathered the more competitive environment by focusing on European markets and enhancing the quality of Tunisian products. The sector contracted 4 percent in 2006, but still represented 5 percent of overall GDP.

Part of the credit for this good health goes to the upgrading program that prepared manufacturing firms for more intense competition. The program hoped to enroll 4,000 firms by 2008. As early as 2001, 2,000 firms had already signed on. By the end of 2006, the total had climbed to 3,896. Of these firms, 2,434 had received approval for their plans to provide additional staff training, to modernize their equipment, or enhance quality control (OECD 2008: 594). Firms that took advantage of the program increased their exports by 13 percent. Thirty-eight percent of them were able to export their goods or services for the first time because of improvements they made through the upgrading program. By the beginning of the twenty-first century, manufactured goods represented 89 percent of Tunisia's exports to Europe.

Other government policies also played an important role in producing Tunisia's return to sound economic health. The central bank's restrictive monetary policy has helped to hold inflation between 3 and 4 percent. The government has continued its policy of steadily expanding exchange rate flexibility, though it does not plan to establish free floating rates before 2009.

The free trade agreement had an immediate impact on foreign investment in Tunisia. In 1990, foreign direct investment (excluding portfolio investments) totaled $70 million. By 2008, foreign investment had climbed to $2.36 billion. Foreign direct investment, as a percentage of GDP, doubled between 1995–2007 (International Monetary Fund 2008a). In 2008, Tunisia's stock of international reserves totaled $8.5 billion, a sum sufficient to cover nearly five months of imports (International Monetary Fund 2008b).

In terms of specific economic sectors, hydrocarbons continue to attract the largest sum of foreign investment, followed by the service and manufacturing industries. British Gas Tunisia's activities make Great Britain the single largest source of foreign investment in Tunisia. Together, European Union countries are responsible for two-thirds of foreign investment. The president of British Gas Tunisia summed up the way many Europeans feel about Tunisia when he said in that 2000 that, "[w]hat we find is that the government is flexible in terms of looking at imaginative ways of developing resources ... One of Tunisia's advantages is that decisions are based on logical and economic drivers" (*Washington Times* 2000). Later, British Gas Tunisia's head of external relations added one other critical draw: "One of the main factors that underpin our partnership is the very sound stability and economic and social predictability that characterize Tunisia. This point is clearly essential for major long-term investment" (Republic of Tunisia 2005). Flexibility, stability, and predictability—these are three of the key values that Tunisia has tried to communicate to global investors.

The remaining third of Tunisia's foreign investment comes from the US and from other Arab countries. There are roughly 200 Arab firms in Tunisia, scattered across a range of activities. While several widely recognized American companies have found their way into Tunisia (including Nabisco,

Pfizer, Citibank), most US investment remains concentrated in the energy sector.[13]

The free trade agreement also boosted the number of foreign firms in Tunisia. In 1973, Tunisia hosted 31 foreign-owned or mixed capital businesses. By 2008, Tunisia was home to more than 2,966 foreign or joint capital firms (Republic of Tunisia 2009). Eighty-five percent of these firms were dedicated entirely to exporting. In the five years immediately following the free-trade agreement, the number of joint ventures doubled and more than 500 new companies decided to invest in Tunisia. The 2009 World Economic Forum's Africa Competitiveness Report declared Tunisia the most competitive of the 31 countries in the study (World Economic Forum 2009).

Challenges for the Future

By any standard, Tunisia has made tremendous economic progress in the five decades since independence. Real per capita incomes have increased more than two and a half times, climbing 40 percent between 2002–5 alone. The official poverty rate has dropped from 40 percent to four percent. Life expectancy has risen from 50 to 73 years. Women now make up a third of the labor force. Over 95 percent of the population has access to potable water and electricity. Primary school enrollment is very close to 100 percent. In 2000, the World Bank declared that Tunisia had "sustained the best economic performance in the Middle East and North Africa region since the late 1980s by maintaining a stable macroeconomic framework and placing strong emphasis on social achievements". It also praised the country for building "the strongest policy and institutional framework for sustainable development in the region" (World Bank 2000: i). On that basis, the World Bank now classifies Tunisia as a lower middle-income country.

Despite this progress, important challenges remain. Unemployment looms as one of the most significant. Between 2002–5, the economy created 282,000 jobs, roughly 70,000 each year. This growth cut one percentage point off the national unemployment rate, but that rate continues to hover stubbornly around 14 percent. This is high compared to many of Tunisia's peers. Persistently high unemployment helps to explain why Tunisia's poverty level did not drop more significantly in the 1990s (African Development Bank 2006: 4). It is important to note that Tunisia needs to do more than produce jobs. It needs to generate high-skilled jobs for the roughly 55,000 new job seekers each year who have university educations.

Education and training reform are one component of the campaign to reduce unemployment. The government has taken important steps to reform vocational and technical education in ways that produce a better fit between the supply and demand curves in the labor market (OECD 2008: 595–7). Tunisia has long boasted high levels of literacy and formal education. But it has not produced sufficient numbers of young people with the specific technical skills that employers need in a rapidly changing economy.

More critical, though, is GDP growth. That will be the most important unemployment sponge. The Tunisian government has said that it wants to catch up with lower-income developed countries like Portugal and South Korea in the first quarter of the twenty-first century. Achieving that goal will require annual growth rates of 8.6 percent from 2005–25 (World Bank 2000: i). At minimum, the economy needs to post growth rates of at least 6 percent in order to continue reducing unemployment.

Currently, the economy cannot generate this kind of growth. Annual GDP growth averaged 5 percent in the 1990s. Since 2000, the economy has hit the 6 percent mark only twice (2004 and 2007). Growth in 2008 only reached 4.6 percent; reduced European demand for Tunisian products in early 2009 will likely translate into lower growth rates at year's end (IMF 2009). There are other sobering statistics. Tunisia's foreign debt has fallen from 65.4 percent of GDP in 2005 to 53.6 at the end of 2007. The government hopes to lower this figure to 46.5 percent by 2009, but even this level would be higher than comparable emerging economies (OECD 2008: 594). Tunisia also continues to run persistent trade and budget deficits.

If Tunisia maintains the policies that it has implemented since the late 1980s, it should be able to sustain the levels of growth that the country has enjoyed in recent years. It will not, however, reach the goals that the government has established for the first quarter of the twenty-first century. Tunisia needs to keep doing what it has been doing for the past twenty years. But it needs to do more of it and to do it more quickly.

For example, exports contributed 45.8 percent of Tunisia's GDP in 2002–5—a good figure, but short of the government's own 47 percent target (African Development Bank 2006: 4). That lag was due primarily to slow growth for two of Tunisia's most important export goods, textiles and leather. These sectors will continue to feel the most intense pressure from freer trade in the region. Both sectors continue to be composed largely of small firms and to struggle with a lack of vertical integration. Similarly, investment growth continues to fall short of government goals. Private investment accounted for 55 percent of total investments in 2002–5. The target was 56 percent. The volume of annual investment growth averaged 2.8 percent during the same period. The government's goal was 7 percent. Foreign direct investment accounted for 2.7 percent of GDP, low in comparison to similar countries. These figures are especially troubling in light of the fact that Tunisia's investment code already offers very generous incentives (ibid.: 3–4). In order to reach the government's growth goals for the 2007–11 period, investment needs to climb from its current 23 percent of GDP to 25.3 percent (World Bank 2008).

Part of the lingering challenge stems from the nature of Tunisia's private sector. Despite nearly five decades of independent development, small, family-owned firms continue to dominate the private sector. One study found that out of 87,000 private firms operating in 1996, only 1,400 employed more than 100 workers. Three-quarters of these companies did less than 1.6 million euros worth of business in a year. Firms with fewer than 20 workers made up more than 60 percent of the industrial sector (Ben Jelili 2005: 26). For the vast majority of private enterprises, survival continues to be more important than growth, so they tend to be very risk-averse. They are hesitant to open their businesses to outside investors. They make small investments in minor projects rather than undertaking more ambitious initiatives that generate growth and jobs.

Additionally, the administrative environment for private businesses, while much improved, continues to discourage and retard growth. The World Bank's *Doing Business 2009* report ranked Tunisia 73rd out of 183 countries in terms of the competitiveness and attractiveness of the business environment. This put Tunisia well ahead of Egypt and Morocco, but still far from what most analysts believe is necessary in order to encourage firms to become more dynamic and to attract new foreign investment (OECD 2008: 594).

Tax breaks and credit opportunities are important, but they alone will not generate long-term commitments to Tunisia's economic growth. These incentives tend to attract volatile capital—money that comes into Tunisia because the investment code offers immediate advantages, but then leaves when another country reforms its code and offers a slightly better deal. Encouraging long-term private sector growth requires a broad environment that makes Tunisia an attractive place to do business. In Tunisia's case, improving physical and technical infrastructure will be vital. Business managers complain about the high costs of internet and international telephone access, about high maritime transportation costs, and about the scarcity of land for industrial site development.

They also complain that the body of regulations for private business remains excessively complex and time-consuming. It can take two to three months to establish a new company in the tourism or agricultural and food industries. Establishing a new manufacturing industry can take up to six months. The same British Gas Tunisia president who praised Tunisia's flexibility also emphasized that "[i]t takes time to get things developed but if one takes the time to understand what the political and strategic requirements are, the analytical and logical approach is one that works well" (*Washington Times* 2000). In an intensely competitive Mediterranean economy, these delays will drive entrepreneurs to other locations. Simplifying the regulatory environment and the civil service that administers it will increase efficiency, reduce the costs of doing business in Tunisia, and reduce the civil service's contribution to the state's wage bill.

Creating new incentives for local firms is one of the most important measures. Since the early 1970s, Tunisia has worked hard to create incentives for export-oriented investment. Between 1975–94, these incentives helped to boost export-oriented investment 15 percent each year. But firms producing for the domestic market have not enjoyed these favors. They pay higher taxes and they face more onerous administrative regulations. They also have a harder time obtaining bank credit. Providing these firms with the same incentives that exporters enjoy will do much to generate fresh dynamism and investment. So, too, will measures that make labor markets more flexible and that encourage banks to make loans to solid small and medium-sized companies.

Perhaps the most critical reforms have as much to do with politics as with economics. Tunisia's economy has changed and grown, in part, because of the government's very close management. President Ben Ali and a small circle of insulated technocrats have done more than design a prudent sequence of reforms. They have micro-managed the day-to-day implementation of those reforms—picking the players, actively shaping the relations between them, cajoling—sometimes threatening—them to behave in ways that support the government's agenda.

To the government's credit, that agenda has reformed the economy in ways that generate growth and distribute it in a reasonably just way. Despite rumors that Ben Ali uses the reform process to line the pockets of political cronies and family members, Tunisia has not suffered from the grotesque corruption that plagues reform in many countries. This is an important asset as the country moves forward.

However, Tunisia has reached the limits of this kind of stage-managed growth. While strong personal stewardship is critical at the outset of the reform process, it leaves that process subject to the interests and will of the stewards. If shifting political winds force leaders to change course, or if the people running the government change, then so do the reforms. These uncertainties drive investors to environments that offer greater stability over longer periods of time.

Consequently, the Tunisian government must replace personal intervention by government officials with clear rules and procedures—depersonalized, transparent institutions that are beyond the politicians' easy reach. Investors, business owners, bankers, workers, consumers, everyone who plays a role in generating economic growth must make decisions in response to clear and consistently-applied rules of the game, not in response to a phone call from a minister or the president. In short, as suggested at the end of the chapter on political development, Tunisia must make more progress toward creating a state of law rather than of man. And just as it does in the political realm, a state of law for the economy requires more players than the government. It requires business interests, consumers, and workers who are able to organize, express their views, and negotiate with government and with each other more freely than they can now.

4 Tunisia and the world

As in many developing countries, domestic issues exert a very strong influence on Tunisia's foreign relations. This is not to say that balances of power, security dilemmas, and other international concerns are unimportant. But for both Bourguiba and Ben Ali, the greatest threats and the most important goals have been domestic. Except for Libya, foreign actors have caused concern not because they threatened to send armies across Tunisia's borders, but because they might work through Tunisian allies to destabilize the government. Both presidents have crafted foreign policies that would thwart these internal-external alliances, maintain the country's independence, attract resources for economic and social development, and ensure strong relationships with France and the US. The result has been a foreign policy that revolves around five essential actors: France, the European Union, the United States, the broader Arab world, and Tunisia's immediate neighbors in the Maghreb.

Tunisia and France

From almost every perspective, Tunisia's single most important foreign relationship has been with France. Even during the most difficult moments of the independence struggle, Bourguiba knew that France would play a vital role in Tunisia's development. For its part, France has wanted to maintain its influence in the region.

Despite these compatible interests, the period from independence to 1970 proved difficult for Franco-Tunisian relations. Tunisia's support for Algeria's independence struggle generated much of the tension in the early years. Economic issues created additional difficulties. While Tunisia became legally independent in 1956, France still dominated the country economically. As noted in the last chapter, French interests continued to own most of the phosphate mines, the fertilizer production facilities, metal works, and glass and paper industries. The French government maintained control of the port and military installations at Bizerte. In 1961, French landowners still held 500,000 hectares of land and controlled large portions of the country's cereal, olive, and wine production. Tunisia conducted 60 percent of its trade with France, and the trade deficit climbed from six billion francs in 1956 to 21 billion in 1960 (Chneguir 2004: 78). This heavy French presence exposed Bourguiba to considerable criticism. He needed to prove that Tunisia was master of its own destiny—and that he was master of Tunisia. The triple challenge of completing Tunisia's economic decolonization, consolidating power, and responding to the economic decline in the 1960s forced Bourguiba to make decisions that unsettled relations with France.

Tensions over Algeria flared immediately after independence. The new government allowed Algerian fighters to operate from bases on Tunisian territory. Tunis became a vital political base for the Algerian nationalist leadership. Fearful that arms would find their way into Algerian hands, France suspended aid and arms sales to Tunisia in 1957. In February 1958, French planes bombed Algerian positions near the Tunisian town of Sakiet Sidi Youssef. The strike killed seventy civilians and injured 150 more. Tunisia recalled its ambassador to France and demanded an immediate timetable for the withdrawal of all French forces from Tunisia—including the port at Bizerte.

France wanted to keep Bizerte because it provided a base from which to monitor a strategic portion of the Mediterranean and to attack eastern Algeria. But it also provided Bourguiba's opponents with a base from which to attack his nationalist credentials. How could Tunisia be truly independent if the former colonial power continued to control a vital port and to maintain military bases in the country? How could Bourguiba allow Tunisian soil to serve as a base for attacks against Algerian nationalists? Bourguiba became particularly angry when he learned in 1960 that France had begun secret negotiations to withdraw its forces from Morocco. How could France insist that it had to keep Bizerte when it was giving up bases elsewhere in the Maghreb?

In the summer of 1961, Bourguiba decided that he had to act more forcefully. Fighting against France violated one of his fundamental goals. He also knew that taking up arms meant certain defeat in military terms. Politically, however, even a lost war could pay important benefits. It would inoculate him against the charge that he was France's lackey, and it would rally domestic and international support for his government. Moreover, Bourguiba hoped that the toll of the Algerian war and the recent crisis in Berlin might make de Gaulle more willing to negotiate France's exit from Bizerte if Tunisia put up a fight. "This is our last quarrel with France", Bourguiba said to a Tunisian emissary who had just returned from a mission to France. "It will cost us dearly", he continued, "but it is the price of deliverance" (Belkhodja 1998: 66).

When France extended a runway at an airbase near Bizerte in July, Bourguiba used it as a pretext to attack France's positions. The fighting lasted a week. It killed 670 Tunisians and wounded 1,555 more. French losses numbered 13 dead and 35 wounded.

Throughout the crisis, Bourguiba remained focused on Tunisia's long-term relationship with France. When thousands demonstrated against France in the streets of Tunis just days before the fighting began, Bourguiba instructed the angry crowd that "we will pursue our fight without hatred or rancor . . . Don't forget that after this crisis . . . we are going to cooperate with France, hand in hand, to defeat underdevelopment" (Belkhodja 1998: 61). When the Arab League proposed an economic boycott of France, Bourguiba rejected the idea (Chneguir 2004: 88).

In two critical respects, Bourguiba's strategy during the Bizerte crisis reflected tactics that had served him well during the independence struggle. Once again, he was playing for regional and international support, presenting France as a colonial occupier and generating additional pressure from abroad. At the same time, however, Bourguiba never lost sight of the fact that France had to be Tunisia's partner after the shooting stopped.

The strategy worked. France agreed to negotiate a timeline for evacuating Bizerte. Governments across the region expressed support for Tunisia's struggle and offered aid. When France evacuated the port in January, 1963, Nasser and Algerian president Ahmed Ben Bella came to Tunis for the event. But less than a year after the Battle of Bizerte, France and Tunisia resumed diplomatic relations and began talks on a series of agreements that enhanced commercial ties and that protected French-owned agricultural land.

Then, in the Spring of 1964, Tunisia suddenly and unilaterally national-ized 350,000 hectares of French land and incorporated them into the state sector (Toumi 1989: 60). France saw the move as a blatant violation of a negotiated accord. Franco-Tunisian relations plunged back into the deep freeze at a time when Bourguiba was about to need powerful friends. In 1965, he angered many across the Arab world by calling for a negotiated settlement between Israel and the Palestinians and by calling on Arab govern-ments to recognize Israel as an unalterable reality. The resulting political isolation made it all the more important for Bourguiba to have external support. But France remained cool. De Gaulle did not trust Bourguiba. He did not like the Tunisian leader's effort to build ties to the US, and he did not like "Bourguibism"—the strategy of achieving goals in successive steps over a prolonged period of time. He thought it made Bourguiba unprincipled and unreliable (Chneguir 2004: 188).

Relations began to thaw in 1966, after Bourguiba publicly conceded that the nationalization had been abrupt and that some could see it as a breach of contract. He described the decision as a regrettable, but unavoidable, product of basic national interest. The economy was deteriorating rapidly and the state needed full command of the country's resources in order to respond as quickly as possible. France also surely recognized that domestic politics played an important role in the decision. Nationalizing French prop-erty contributed to Bourguiba's effort to protect himself from Tunisia's increasingly vocal left. If some French leaders were unhappy with him, at the end of the day he was better than the alternatives.

Relations improved more dramatically after de Gaulle's resignation in

1969 (ibid.: 123–4). As domestic political conflicts and tensions with Libya escalated over the course of the 1970s and 1980s, French support for Bourguiba and for Tunisia's sovereignty became critically important. The two governments established a stronger framework for regular consultation, and the Franco-Tunisian Chamber of Commerce and Industry played a vital role in expanding commercial relations between the two countries. France became Tunisia's primary supplier and its second customer. Per person, French aid to Tunisia climbed to the highest level of assistance from one country to another in the world. Cultural, economic, and technical cooperation expanded dramatically over the course of the 1970s.

France also became the primary guarantor of Tunisia's security. In the early 1970s, France lifted its prohibition on the sale of weapons to Tunisia. Paris later expanded Tunisia's right to purchase any French weapon it wanted for its defense. France also provided extensive training for Tunisia's military and internal security forces. These commitments to arm, train, and reinforce Tunisian forces became particularly critical as tensions with Libya increased in the 1980s. In May, 1986, Jacques Chirac, then Prime Minister in François Mitterand's government, publicly declared that

> France and Tunisia are two countries whose ties are such that whatever affects one affects the other immediately . . . If Tunisia was the victim of any kind of aggression, and if it wanted France's help, France would provide it instantly and without reservation.
>
> (Chneguir 2004: 191)

Despite these close economic and military ties, France and Tunisia struggled through another difficult period in the 1990s. Echoing the early years after Tunisia's independence, conflict in Algeria helped to generate this tension. Governments in Paris and Tunis feared that the battle between the Algerian government and the Islamic Salvation Front (FIS) would spill across the border into Tunisia. Paris had little to say about Ben Ali's crackdown on Ennahdha. But as it became clearer that he was taking a hard line against all forms of opposition and criticism, the French press and substantial portions of the left became vocal critics. This was particularly true after Lionel Jospin became France's prime minister in 1997 (Ghorbal 2003: 89–90).

Due in large part to this criticism, the European Parliament passed resolutions expressing concern about human rights in Tunisia in 1996 and twice in 2002. In 1996, Ben Ali delayed a scheduled trip to Paris until the following year in order to avoid public criticism. His government banned several French newspapers and France 2 television for a period of time in 1999. When the Ben Brik affair in 2000 provided the French press with another opportunity to complain about media control in Tunisia, Ben Ali responded by reopening the debate about the status of the French language in Tunisia. The French Socialist Party froze relations with Tunisia's ruling RCD in 2001.

These incidents complicated relations between Paris and Tunis, but as a former French ambassador to Tunis noted, "the core of the relationship never was in danger" (Ghorbal 2003: 90). French officials occasionally have issued carefully worded statements about the importance of human rights and the rule of law. But they have never taken stronger measures because, in the final analysis, Ben Ali's value as a leader who maintains stability and encourages economic development trumps concerns about his authoritarianism. Indeed, France increased its aid to Tunisia on several occasions over the course of the 1990s. When Ben Ali visited Paris in 1997, the two governments signed agreements that provided funds to support French investments and the modernization of Tunisian businesses. *Jeune Afrique* described the accord, which contained terms very favorable to Tunisia, as the first of its kind signed with a Mediterranean country (Wood 2002: 100).

At the dawn of the new century, "France remained Tunisia's primary commercial partner, and Tunisia is one of only four countries (Algeria, Morocco, Vietnam) that benefit from all French development-aid programs" (ibid.: 104). Politically, too, Franco-Tunisian relations have improved. Tunisia's position during the 2003 Gulf War coincided closely with France's. President Jacques Chirac worked very hard in the first decade of the new millennium to improve France's relations with all of the Maghreb states. Unlike François Mitterand, who pushed hard—and unsuccessfully—for greater unity in the Maghreb, Chirac focused on improving bilateral relations between France and each of the region's governments. As much as Tunisia advocates closer cooperation between Maghrebi governments, it also likes not having its relationship with France freighted down with Algerian or Moroccan issues. As discussed below, Chirac's successor, Nicolas Sarkozy, has also tried to reach across the Mediterranean and build stronger ties to the Maghreb.

This bilateralism reflects a pragmatic understanding of the region's politics. As discussed later in this chapter, the Maghreb states will not develop unified policies about any issue of great significance anytime soon. But it also reflects France's desire to remain the most important external player in the Maghreb at a time when US influence has increased substantially. That desire, however, must contend with globalization and the finite resources that constrain all governments. Immigration, economic integration, and shared security concerns have turned most Franco-Tunisian issues into Euro-Maghreb issues. Consequently, Franco-Tunisian relations have developed in the broader context of relations between the northern and southern shores of the Mediterranean.

Tunisia and Europe

The European Economic Community began developing formal economic ties to the southern Mediterranean in the late 1960s. The goal was to negotiate agreements that increased southern Mediterranean exports to

Europe and gradually opened those economies to freer trade. Tunisia signed an association agreement with the EEC in 1969.

These accords reflected noble goals, but they fell short of expectations. They made it easier for Maghrebi countries to export manufactured goods to Europe, but these goods made up only 7–8 percent of Tunisia's total exports at that time. Most of Tunisia's manufacturing sector produced for local consumption. Many other industrial goods did not qualify for advantages because they violated one of the many technical rules contained in the terms of the agreement. For example, rules regarding exports to Europe excluded goods produced by joint projects between Tunisia and other countries. Although Europe imported some mining and petroleum products from Tunisia, the customs duties on these goods remained too low to generate substantial income. Additionally, the 1969 agreement protected European agricultural producers and prevented Tunisia from finding European markets for its olive oil and other leading agricultural exports. Despite an additional accord in 1976 that involved greater European investment in infrastructure, production, research, and promotion activities, Tunisia's trade deficit with Europe continued to grow (Chneguir 2004: 156–60, 213–21).

Tunisia's case exemplified a broader trend. Across the board, these early agreements between the EEC and southern Mediterranean countries failed to boost trade between the regions as dramatically as many hoped. While the volume of trade between the two regions grew in absolute terms, each region's share of the goods in the other's overall trade balance remained stable. In other words, although southern Mediterranean countries sold more to Europe, those goods did not conquer a larger portion of European markets. While Europe accounted for roughly half of the imports and exports in the southern Mediterranean region, the southern Mediterranean represented only three percent of Europe's total imports and exports (Nsouli *et al.* 1996: 14). Other countries continued to enjoy much larger shares of European markets.

Much of the challenge for Tunisia and other Maghreb countries stemmed from the entry of Spain, Greece, and Portugal into the EEC in the late 1970s. These countries produced many of the same agricultural products as the Maghreb. Their entry into the EEC meant that their products enjoyed protected access to other European markets. This, in turn, made it even more difficult for Maghreb countries to find European markets for their primary export goods.

Spurred by deepening concerns about political instability, economic stagnation, and immigration, the European Union and twelve Mediterranean countries signed the Euro-Mediterranean Partnership Initiative in November, 1995. Known widely as the Barcelona Process, the initiative tried to create a truly regional framework for managing a range of socio-economic issues.

Barcelona's centerpiece was a series of new association agreements negotiated between the EU and individual southern Mediterranean countries.

These agreements gave Middle Eastern and North African countries greater access to European markets. However, they also required these countries to progressively lower tariffs on European industrial goods. To help Mediterranean countries prepare for this transition, the EU pledged aid to help them upgrade their manufacturing sectors. The EU hoped that these bilateral agreements would lay the foundation for a huge industrial free trade zone by 2010. Tunisia took great pride in becoming the first Maghreb country to sign an association agreement in 1995. Ben Ali saw it as Europe's validation of his economic and security policies.

As discussed in the last chapter, the agreement called for a twelve-year transition to a free-trade zone between Tunisia and the EU. Tunisia would receive free access to EU markets for manufactured goods. In turn, Tunisia would have to eliminate all tariff and non-tariff barriers to industrial imports from EU countries. The plan also called for dialogue on a range of social issues, including immigration, and for a progressive harmonization of Tunisian and EU regulatory frameworks governing a range of economic activities.

Despite the lofty rhetoric and the clear need for a regional approach to regional challenges, the 1995 Barcelona Accord never lived up to expectations on either side of the Mediterranean. Conflict in the Middle East stymied progress in the eastern Mediterranean. In the Maghreb, slow economic growth, conflict in Algeria, and competition between countries in the region prevented meaningful progress toward greater economic cooperation. While governments talked a great deal about building economic ties across the Maghreb, they continued to look north more often than east or west. At the end of the day, each of them believed that economic ties to European countries would boost growth more quickly than ties to their neighbors.

North African leaders never denied these problems, but they also argued that European countries deserved a large portion of the blame. As one Algerian official put it, "The Europeans decide almost everything . . . They chose the projects, the levels and the modes of financing. This put the Mediterranean at the periphery rather than the center of Europe" (Hani 2008b). Maghrebi officials felt that Europeans never delivered the investment or the project financing that they promised. As a result, more than a decade after the Barcelona agreement was signed, the economic disparity between the northern and southern shores of the Mediterranean was greater than the disparity between any two other contiguous regions. Only 2 percent of Europe's investment went to the southern Mediterranean. This represented a very small investment from governments that expressed strong concerns about immigration. Economists estimated in 2008 that Maghrebi economies would have to create forty million new jobs over the next 10–15 years simply to maintain current levels of unemployment (Zahar, 2008).

Leaders on both sides of the Mediterranean have tried to address these problems with the Barcelona Process. In May, 2003 the EU's European

Neighborhood Policy expanded the areas of cooperation between the two regions. In 2004, Tunisia and nine other countries (Algeria, Libya, Morocco, Mauritania, Spain, France, Italy, Malta, and Portugal) signed a Mediterranean "5+5" security agreement for increased military cooperation (Coustillière 2005).

The most significant new proposal came in 2007, when French President Nicolas Sarkozy proposed a Mediterranean Union that would create a more genuine partnership between the countries that ring the Mediterranean. Tunisia was one of the initiative's first and most enthusiastic supporters, in part because Tunis was a candidate home for the Union's headquarters (Hani 2008b). But German and EU officials objected to the Union's exclusion of non-Mediterranean European states. Given Europe's high degree of integration, they argued that it made no sense to address immigration, security, or economic development issues on such narrow geographic terms. All of the members of the EU should be members of the Union, not only those with Mediterranean coastlines. German and EU officials also saw Sarkozy's initiative as an effort to project France as the most important European player in the Middle East and North Africa. France agreed to incorporate all of the EU members and the organization was renamed the Union for the Mediterranean.

In spite of this demonstrated will, the idea of a partnership between Europe and its Maghreb neighbors faces several daunting challenges. Bringing all of the EU's members into the Union for the Mediterranean could hobble the effort. The number of members and the diversity of their interests and priorities could mean that southern Mediterranean issues get lost in the midst of the other pressing issues facing Europe. Then there is the issue of money. How much will European members be willing to commit to support Mediterranean projects (Simons 2008)?

The prospects for collective action are no better on the southern shore. As discussed later in this chapter, the countries of the Maghreb have a very difficult time cooperating with each other. It is difficult to see them developing any common strategy or program for their relationship with Europe in the near future. Lacking any concerted approach, the Union could change very little about relations between the Maghreb and Europe. Individual Maghreb countries could simply continue to compete with one another to see who can negotiate the best deals with Europe and attract the most development assistance funds. It is hard to use terms like "partnership" or "union" to describe that kind of future.

Tunisia and the United States

Although Tunisia's diplomatic relations with the United States began shortly after American independence, little of consequence transpired between the two countries until the 1940s, when the politics of the Second World War intersected with the politics of Tunisian nationalism. As discussed earlier, many Arab nationalists expressed sympathy for the Axis because a German victory over Britain and France might hasten the end of colonial rule. Bourguiba's support for Gaullist France made Tunisia a notable exception.

It also put Tunisian nationalism on the side of the new global power that could pressure France after the war—the US. Knowing that external support would be critical to his effort to get France out of Tunisia, Bourguiba worked to establish strong ties with the United States during the war years.

The US did encourage France to negotiate with the Neo-Destour. But the intensification of the Cold War in the late 1940s and 1950s created a powerful dilemma for the US. On the one hand, Washington was very concerned about the spread of communism in Asia and Africa. Bourguiba's unabashed support for the West and his criticism of Nasser and pan-Arabism made him a useful ally in a critical region. On the other hand, France was a NATO ally and a key protector of Western interests in the Mediterranean. Maintaining good relations with both required some difficult decisions.

When France suspended arms sales to Tunisia in 1957, the Eisenhower administration criticized the decision as short-sighted. As an independent state, Tunisia had a right to arm itself. If France did not sell the weapons, the US feared that Bourguiba might buy them from Nasser or the Soviets. Additionally, taking such a hard line with Tunis might undermine France's position in the Maghreb and its ability to defend Western interests in the Mediterranean. To pressure France and keep Tunisia tied to the West, the US and Great Britain vowed to sell arms to Tunisia if Paris would not.

During the Bizerte crisis in 1961, however, the US refused to support Tunisia as vigorously as Bourguiba wanted. Tunisia took its case to the United Nations and called for a vote condemning France's occupation of the port. President Kennedy sent Bourguiba a note saying that in light of the recent crisis in Berlin, he could not vote for Tunisia's resolution. His concern about the fragile political balance in Europe would not allow him to openly condemn an important NATO ally (Chneguir 2004: 83).

Despite this hesitancy to take sides publicly in spats between France and Tunisia, the US proved very willing to become Tunisia's most important source of economic assistance after France. The US and Tunisia signed their first bilateral agreement on economic and technical assistance in 1957. The US Agency for International Development (USAID) maintained a very successful program in Tunisia until 1994, when Tunisia reached a level of development beyond the need for the program's funding. From 1957–84, USAID assistance accounted for nearly one-sixth of Tunisia's income. This support was particularly critical in the 1960s, when France cut or eliminated aid because of the conflicts over Bizerte and the nationalization of French-owned land. In 1960–69, US food aid to Tunisia totaled $316 million (Friends of Tunisia 2006).

The US also provided substantial military assistance to Tunisia during periods of heightened tension with Libya. From Washington's perspective, this economic and military aid constituted an investment in a stable leader who pursued progressive, pro-Western policies in an unsettled region. From Bourguiba's perspective, the US provided an additional Western guarantor of Tunisia's economic development and military security, a source to which Tunisia could turn—or threaten to turn—during periods of difficulty with France.

US-Tunisian relations developed a new intimacy after Ben Ali took power in 1987. Washington quickly expressed its support for Tunisia's new president. The US had developed serious doubts about Bourguiba's ability to manage the country's mounting political and economic crises. Policymakers in Washington were pleased to see Ben Ali provide a decisive answer to the succession question and to hear his pledge of support for liberal economic and political reform.

Economic issues account for some of the closeness between Washington and Ben Ali. Since the early 1990s, globalization and market-oriented reforms have turned the Mediterranean basin into an attractive and competitive marketplace. The US has worked diligently to expand trade within the Maghreb and to create new opportunities for US businesses there. In 1998 the Clinton administration launched the US-North Africa Economic Partnership. Known commonly as the Eizenstat Initiative, the program encouraged economic integration between Tunisia, Algeria, and Morocco. The goal was to create a larger consumer market (some 80 million consumers in the three countries) that would enhance trade, attract US investment to the region and, according to some, challenge the EU's domination of the Maghreb's external economic relations. The program provided more than $4 million in assistance to Tunisia from 2001–3 (US Department of State March 2009). In 2002, the US folded the Eizenstat projects into a new Middle East Partnership Initiative and added new bilateral and regional projects that support education reform, civil society development, and women's empowerment initiatives.

Tunisia's stability, location, and commitment to export-driven development make it a valuable partner in America's effort to expand economic ties to the region. In addition to opportunities inside Tunisia itself, the country's location makes it a useful "market relay" to nearby European, African, and Asian markets. In 2002, the US and Tunisia signed a Trade and Investment Framework Agreement (TIFA). TIFAs are intended to strengthen bilateral ties as stepping stones to eventual free trade agreements. By 2007, nearly 70 US corporations had a presence in Tunisia with investments totaling $750 million. These investments have created approximately 18,000 jobs in Tunisia (Abrouq 2008). Despite this progress, the US still is not a major economic partner for Tunisia. Europe still accounts for more than 70 percent of Tunisia's foreign trade. In fact, by 2008, the US had fallen to eighth place on the list of Tunisia's suppliers.

More than economics, security concerns provide the most powerful cement in contemporary US–Tunisian relations. From the US perspective, Tunisia's location allows it to play a role in two critical regions. Tunisia is a

"Middle Eastern" country insofar as it is part of the arc of predominantly Muslim countries in North Africa, the Middle East, and West Asia that face similar challenges: young and growing populations, fragile economies, bipolar political landscapes that pit authoritarian governments against Islamist parties that have eclipsed secular parties as the most popular opposition voices.

At the same time, Tunisia and its Maghreb neighbors are "African" countries. They provide the buffer between Europe and the band of deeply troubled countries that spans the African Sahel and Horn—Mauritania, Mali, Niger, Chad, Sudan, Somalia, Eritrea, and Ethiopia. By the mid-1990s, disease, ethnic conflict, dire poverty, and state collapse had turned the region into a belt of misery. Beyond humanitarian concerns, the United States fears that instability in the region could jeopardize access to strategic resources—oil, manganese, cobalt, chrome, vanadium, gold, antimony, fluorspar, germanium, and industrial diamonds. Chronic instability could also spawn Islamist movements similar to those in the Middle East and western Asia.

Shared concerns about regional stability have provided the foundation for a mutually beneficial relationship between Tunis and Washington. Even before the September 11 attacks, the US held more joint military exercises with Tunisia than with any other Mediterranean country (Zoubir and Zunes 1999: 238). In addition to standing as a bulwark against Islamism, Tunisia has provided the US with valuable intelligence about Islamist networks in North Africa and Europe. Ben Ali has expressed support for US operations in Afghanistan, and it was widely rumored that Tunisian, Algerian, and Moroccan agents worked with US forces to identify insurgents who entered Iraq from other Arabic-speaking countries after Saddam Hussein's fall in 2003. Ben Ali could have a very strong personal interest in the US effort there. According to some sources, unnamed authorities arrested more than 600 Tunisians between 2005–7 as they tried to travel to Iraq (Smith 2007). Tunisia has also discussed the possibility of building bases in the southern part of the country that the US could use to pre-position troops and supplies for use in the Middle East or sub-Saharan Africa.

In return for this cooperation, American supplies and training have greatly enhanced Tunisia's security and intelligence services. While the US has long provided this kind of support, it has become even more important in the post-September 11 period. In 2005, Tunisia was one of nine countries incorporated into a new Trans-Sahara Counter-terrorism Initiative. The Trans-Sahara Initiative reflected Washington's desire to avoid direct involvement in the region by helping local governments work together more effectively to combat threats to stability. But the agreement also includes non-military components. The US Department of State will help to improve airport security. USAID will build schools. The US Treasury Department will help governments improve their ability to track the flow of money through their countries.

The US has also provided Ben Ali with important political support. President George H. W. Bush invited Ben Ali to the White House in 1989 and 1990. Secretary of State Warren Christopher visited Tunisia in 1993. First Lady Hillary Clinton visited in 1999. Secretary of State Colin Powell came to Tunisia in 2004 to thank Tunisia for its role in convincing Libya to abandon its quest for unconventional weapons. These public expressions of support have bolstered Ben Ali's credibility at home and abroad by demonstrating that the US considers Tunisia an important regional player.

There have been moments of tension. Relations chilled after Israeli forces bombed PLO headquarters in Tunis in 1985 and after they assassinated a high-ranking PLO official in 1988. There have been substantive disagreements. Ben Ali wanted to end Libya's diplomatic isolation in the late 1980s and early 1990s while Washington preferred to maintain pressure on Qadhafi. The US also grumbled about Ben Ali's support for Iraq during the first Gulf War in 1990–91. Finally, American officials have expressed concern about some of Ben Ali's methods. But they have done so quietly, and they have avoided broad condemnations of the government as a whole. Most of the criticism has focused on issues of individual rights and liberties (particularly freedom of the press) rather than on the general system of government. But neither government has allowed these issues to weaken the core of their relationship.

In general terms, then, America's role in Tunisian foreign policy has changed relatively little since 1956. As Zoubir and Zones put it, "[t]he main characteristic of US-Tunisian relations is constancy" (1999: 237). While the security component has become more important over the past decade, the general themes and tenor of the relationship have remained consistent. From Bourguiba through Ben Ali, Tunisia has courted the US as its second major Western source of military and economic support. As the following section describes, both presidents have been willing to do this even though it has generated serious tension with their neighbors.

Tunisia and the Middle East

Like many countries in the Middle East and North Africa, dealing with neighbors has been Tunisia's greatest foreign policy challenge. Three specific issues have complicated Tunisia's relations within the region. The first is Tunisia's resolute commitment to Tunisian nationalism and its resistance to any kind of pan-Arab or pan-Maghreb nationalism that would erode Tunisia's sovereignty. The second is Tunisia's position on the conflict between Israel and the Palestinians. Relations with Algeria and Libya have been the third source of tension. We will deal with that issue in the following section on the Maghreb.

Conflicts between pan-Arab nationalism and Tunisian nationalism date to at least the late 1940s. Many Maghrebi nationalists argued that France was too strong for any of their movements to win alone. In 1947, the leading nationalist parties, including the Neo-Destour, pledged to wage a unified struggle for independence across the region. Bourguiba broke this pledge when he decided to negotiate with France for Tunisia's internal autonomy and independence.

That commitment to a specifically Tunisian nationalism contributed to Bourguiba's split with the Youssefist wing of the party. It created more difficulties in the 1950s and 1960s, when much of the Arab world was in the thrall of pan-Arabism and Egypt's president Gamal Abd al-Nasser. Beyond his personal suspicion of Nasser, Bourguiba believed that pan-Arabism—the idea that all Arabs should join together to eliminate borders and create one huge state—was romantic nonsense that ignored the very real historical, political, cultural, and economic differences between countries. Given Tunisia's small size and lack of resources, joining a pan-Arab union would mean surrendering Tunisia's independence to Nasser's ambitions. Bourguiba had no intention of trading French overlords for Egyptian ones. The short-lived United Arab Republic (1958–61), a "union" that allowed Nasser to essentially take over Syria, confirmed Bourguiba's suspicions.

Bourguiba's vocal skepticism of pan-Arabism and Nasser created serious tensions between the Tunisian and Egyptian governments through the 1960s. Nasser lambasted Bourguiba on Egypt's powerful *Sawt al-Arab* radio and openly supported his Youssefist opponents. Particularly after Qadhafi came to power in Libya as a pan-Arab nationalist in 1969, Bourguiba feared that Tunisia would get caught between Libya and Algeria—two large, oil-rich states with pan-Arab sympathies and close ties to Nasser.

By that point, however, the Palestinian issue had begun to generate even more tension between Bourguiba and most of the Arab world. Bourguiba saw Palestine, like Algeria, as a victim of settler colonialism. Bourguiba had been in Egypt during the first Arab-Israeli war in 1948–49. The Arab defeat in that war and again in 1956 gave him a keen appreciation for Israel's military strength. On the basis of the objective military balance, Bourguiba argued that Palestinians could not depend on the Arab states to win Palestine in a conventional war. Palestinians would have to do what Algerians and Tunisians had done. They would have to take responsibility for their own liberation and organize a combined guerrilla and political campaign. The goal of that campaign should not be to push Israel out of Palestine. Palestinians would never be able to muster the strength to do that. The goal must be to rally international support and to sow enough uncertainty and fear to make Israel choose to negotiate a settlement. The Arab states could support the struggle by providing safe havens for Palestinian fighters, just as Tunisia had done for the FLN. A tour of Palestinian refugee camps in Jordan in 1964 only strengthened Bourguiba's commitment to this strategy. While he never questioned the rightness of the Palestinian cause, the conditions he saw in the camps convinced Bourguiba that Palestinians could not simply fight their way to freedom (Chneguir 2004: 100–1).

Bourguiba made this case in a March, 1965 speech in Jericho. He had gone there as part of a regional tour. In very pointed language, Bourguiba said that Palestinians continued to sustain themselves with "chimerical hopes and sterile hatreds". He said that this toxic blend of anger and romanticism had impeded "all lucid action" by Palestinians and other Arab governments (ibid.: 101). Palestinians had to develop a more nuanced and realistic strategy. They should exploit the fact that most of the international community supported their cause. Successive UN resolutions made this support clear. Palestinians should wage as much of the struggle as possible through legal means, and root their position in UN Resolutions 181 (November 1947) and 194 (December 1948). Those resolutions called for a division of Palestine into Jewish and Palestinian states, with a clear right of return for Palestinian refugees. Accepting Israel's existence and basing their strategy on UN decisions would put Palestinian nationalism on the side of international law. If Israel would not accept these same resolutions, including a Palestinian state, then Israel clearly would become an international outlaw. International pressure would have to play a vital role in the effort to establish a Palestinian state. Violence had to be used strategically. Like the Neo-Destour, Palestinians should calibrate its use carefully to push Israel to the negotiating table (Mahjoubi 2004).

Grounded in a clear-eyed assessment of the balance of forces, and supported by Tunisia's own successful struggle against France, Bourguiba's advice commanded serious attention. Indeed, some Israeli politicians feared that Arab leaders might take it. But Israel's Prime Minister at the time, David Ben Gurion, was not concerned. "Don't worry", he said. "Our adversaries here are different. There's no chance that they will take a bourguibist approach" (ibid.: 79).

Bourguiba's speech, and Tunisia's refusal to break ties with West Germany when it recognized Israel, ignited a wave of anti-Tunisian anger across the region. Suggesting that the Arab states could not defeat Israel and calling for a negotiated solution in Palestine bordered on heresy in the 1960s. Governments in Egypt, Syria, and Iraq drew much of their legitimacy from their commitment to confrontation with Israel. Rumors of assassination plots forced Bourguiba to cancel the rest of his tour. Angry crowds burned the Tunisian chancellery in Cairo while police stood by. Marchers in streets across the region burned Bourguiba in effigy. Some unrest even broke out in Tunisia. Bourguiba temporarily broke off relations with the Arab League in 1965 and with Egypt the following year.

The catastrophic Arab defeat in June 1967 proved Bourguiba and Ben Gurion right. Nasser and pan-Arabism never recovered from those six days. That defeat, and Nasser's death in 1970, eliminated one of Bourguiba's greatest concerns.

By the early 1970s, Tunisian diplomacy had gained a reputation far beyond the country's modest size. It enjoyed wide respect as a producer of skilled diplomats and careful, pragmatic policy advisors. In addition to its role in Algeria, Tunisia had played a helpful role in several African countries' transitions to independence. Tunisia's Prime Minister in 1970, Bahi Ladgham, received widespread praise for his skilled mediation of the Black September conflict between Jordan and the Palestine Liberation Organization (PLO) (Toumi 1989: 74–5).

Despite this reputation, Tunisia did not play a powerful role in Middle Eastern issues in the 1970s. The country was consumed by its own internal conflicts. As we will discuss later, relations with Algeria and Libya became Tunisia's principal foreign policy concerns.

At the end of the decade, though, Middle Eastern affairs came to Tunis. When Egypt signed the Camp David Accords with Israel in 1979, the Arab League responded by moving its headquarters from Cairo to Tunis. When the PLO left Beirut in 1983, it moved to Tunis, as well, to be near the heart of the region's diplomatic activity. Hosting these organizations enhanced Bourguiba's and Ben Ali's regional credibility at a time when both leaders needed it badly. It also raised Tunisia's profile in diplomatic circles beyond the Arab world. Since Tunis was the location for dialogue with the Arab League and the PLO, it became a more important diplomatic posting than it had been in the past. Many governments posted their best ambassadorial talent with strong regional expertise to Tunisia in the 1980s. The League moved back to Cairo after Egypt was readmitted in 1989. The PLO left Tunis after signing the 1993 Oslo Accords with Israel.

The First Gulf War in 1990 put Ben Ali in a difficult position. It was difficult to side against an ally as important as the US. But Tunisian public opinion ran strongly in Iraq's favor, and Ben Ali was still trying to consolidate power. His methods for dealing with political opposition, particularly the Islamists, had begun to tarnish his early image as a democratic reformer. With Tunisians marching in the streets against the US, he had little choice but to take Iraq's side. There was less tension between the US and Tunisia over the Second Gulf War in 2003. After the fall of Saddam Hussein's government, Tunisia led the Arab League's effort to assemble a force that would protect the United Nations offices in Baghdad.

The following year, however, Tunisia became embroiled in a serious Arab League controversy. The League had scheduled its annual summit to open in Tunis at the end of March. In the weeks leading up to the summit, two issues began to generate serious discord within the League's membership. The first was the Middle East peace process. Many members, including Tunisia, wanted to use the summit to restart stalled negotiations between Israel and the Palestinians. Other members remained less enthusiastic, particularly in the immediate wake of the assassination of Hamas founder Sheikh Yassin.

Proposals for political reform in the Middle East provided the more important source of conflict. As part of its campaign to promote democracy as an antidote to Islamism, the Bush administration had begun to press Arab governments more vigorously for reforms that would democratize political processes across the region, create new opportunities for women, protect human rights, and ensure basic liberties. These ideas lay at the core a new

Greater Middle East Initiative that the US wanted to present to the members of the G8 in June 2004. Some members of the League wanted the organization to take a clear stand in favor of these principles. Others resisted, either because they opposed the substance of these measures, or because they did not like the idea of adopting a reform agenda that had been prepared by the US. Less than two days before the summit was scheduled to open, Ben Ali unilaterally decided to postpone it. The move came as a surprise to governments across the region. Publicly, the Tunisian government said that its own commitments to modernization and to the liberation of women would not allow it to host a summit that did not take these ideas seriously. Others in the region suggested that Ben Ali was concerned that an open call for political reform would embarrass his own government (Abu Odeh 2004).

Whatever his motives, Ben Ali's decision to postpone the summit made him the target of criticism across the region. After considerable haggling, the summit took place on May 23–24. All 22 Arab League states were represented, but Bahrain, the UAE, Saudi Arabia, Sudan, Oman, and Yemen did not send their heads of state as a protest over the agenda. The resulting Declaration of Tunis called for reforming and modernizing the Arab world by consolidating democratic practices. It also called for expanding women's participation in social, economic and political life and reinforcing women's rights.

The Maghreb

Of all Tunisia's foreign relationships, none have been more complicated than those with its most immediate neighbors. It is not surprising that proximity might breed conflict, but Maghreb unity has been a hallowed staple in the region's political vocabulary since the 1920s. The core of the region—Tunisia, Algeria, and Morocco—is richly endowed with characteristics that make extensive cooperation seem inevitable: cultural homogeneity, a shared French colonial experience, broad-based nationalist movements that cooperated extensively during the struggles for independence, the challenges of globalization and an economically unified Europe. Proclaiming faith in at least the idea of some sort of union or federation has long been part of the ritualized rhetoric of Maghrebi relations.

Despite these factors, suspicion and self-interest have dominated the region's politics and repeatedly hobbled efforts at multilateral cooperation. Tunisia's small size and narrow resource base have made it the most consistent supporter of close cooperation, particularly on economic issues. But these same characteristics also have given Tunisia the strongest reasons to fear domination by its neighbors.

In the years immediately following independence, Algeria posed the greatest regional foreign policy challenge for Tunisia. As discussed earlier, Algeria's fight for independence complicated Tunisia's relationship with

France. The internal politics of the Algerian revolution created additional challenges. The Algerian nationalist movement was not a unified entity. Political and military leaders who operated from Tunisia and Morocco struggled for control with each other and with the military commanders who led the fighting inside Algeria. In this struggle, Bourguiba supported the Provisional Government of the Algerian Republic in its effort to negotiate a settlement with France. After the Provisional Government negotiated the Evian Accords that gave Algeria its independence in 1962, army officers imposed one of their own, Ahmed Ben Bella, as the country's first president. Ben Bella's faction shared Nasser's pan-Arab sympathies. Like Nasser, they were suspicious of Bourguiba and supported the Youssefist opposition inside Tunisia. Along with disputes about the contours of the Algeria-Tunisia border, these suspicions lingered after another coup brought Houari Boumedienne to power as Algeria's president in 1965. The two governments resolved their border dispute in 1970 and negotiated nearly fifty economic and technical agreements over the next five years. One of the most important involved a gas pipeline that connected Algeria to Italy by way of Tunisia.

Nevertheless, relations between the two governments remained tense. Boumedienne feared that Tunisia, with its explicitly pro-Western posture, might become a source of instability on Algeria's eastern flank. Bourguiba remained leery of Algeria's size, its hydrocarbon wealth, its military, and its revolutionary philosophy (Belkhodja 1998: 169).

Over the course of the 1970s, however, Libya became Tunisia's most serious concern. Muammar Qadhafi seized power in 1969 as an unabashed pan-Arab nationalist. Initially, Tunisia and Libya cooperated on a range of economic and social issues. The two economies complemented each other well. Libya enjoyed extensive hydrocarbon resources and wanted to rapidly modernize its infrastructure. But it lacked a large, well-educated workforce—a resource that Tunisia enjoyed in abundance. Libya's development needs provided opportunities for Tunisian companies and a sponge for Tunisian unemployment. In the early 1970s, the two governments established mixed companies in the manufacturing, maritime transport, and construction sectors. In return, Libya invested heavily in Tunisia's Fourth Development Plan (Chneguir 2004: 175).

These ties created the most extensive economic relationship between any two Maghrebi states. But they were not strong enough to withstand the fundamental political differences between the two governments. After Nasser's death in 1970, Qadhafi presented himself as the region's next great pan-Arab hero. Drawing other states into a union under Libya's leadership would make it the region's dominant power. In less than two decades, Qadhafi pursued at least seven different unity plans with various partners (Vandewalle 2006: 87).

Between 1972 and 1974, Tunisia became the fulcrum in the balance of power in the Maghreb. In December, 1972, Qadhafi visited Tunis and delivered an impassioned plea for union with Libya. Such a union would serve several goals. Qadhafi feared that the Algeria–Tunisia–Italy gas pipeline would pull Tunisia into Algeria's orbit. Binding Tunisia to Libya would tip the balance of power in Libya's favor and expand Qadhafi's plans for a union with Egypt and Syria. It also would domesticate a US and French ally in the region and thwart any other Maghreb unity plan. Like Nasser, Qadhafi dismissed any specifically Maghreb union plan as a schismatic deviation from true pan-Arabism (Toumi 1989: 91; Belkhodja 1998: 192). Bourguiba delivered a sharp reply to Qadhafi's sermon. He chided Qadhafi for his youthful naivete and he argued that governments must pursue any union prudently and over a prolonged period of time.

Watching from the west, the Algerians felt compelled to block Qadhafi's bid for regional dominance. Boumedienne proposed an Algerian union with Tunisia when he met with Bourguiba in May, 1973. Again, Bourguiba resisted the idea of a union that risked submitting Tunisia to domination by one of its large, oil-rich neighbors (Belkhodja 1998: 171–2).

Then, less than a year later, in one of the most perplexing moments in Tunisia's political history, Bourguiba suddenly agreed to a union with Libya. There had been none of the planning and consultation that Bourguiba insisted should precede any union. There was no prior discussion of the plan within the top circles of Tunisia's ruling party. Qadhafi met Bourguiba on the island of Djerba, and after a brief conversation, Bourguiba signed a treaty that Qadhafi had written by hand on a piece of paper. The agreement established the Arab Islamic Republic. Bourguiba would be president; Qadhafi would control the armed forces.

Observers have offered a range of explanations for the sudden about-face. Some blame Bourguiba, either because his deteriorating health allowed Qadhafi to manipulate him or because his ego would not allow him to walk away from the opportunity to preside over such a large state. Others suggest that Qadhafi exploited the deepening divisions in Tunisia's political elite by offering high positions in the new unionist government to officials who would help bring Tunisia into the union (Toumi 1989: 90–8; Belkhodja 1998: 202).

These explanations present Qadhafi as the union's sole architect. But there is another possibility, one that involves Bourguiba as a more active player in the game. According to at least one memoir, Bourguiba actually encouraged Qadhafi to consider a union with Tunisia when he visited Tripoli in September, 1973—four months prior to the Djerba union. At the time, Qadhafi was dispirited that his plan for a union with Egypt had collapsed. Bourguiba is reported to have told Qadhafi, "They're all Levantines in the Middle East . . . I never believed in your union with Egypt. Come to Tunisia and things will be more serious" (Belkhodja 1998: 197).

Why might Bourguiba, a leader who so consistently rejected any form of union, suddenly encourage it? It is conceivable, and entirely consistent with his pragmatism, that he decided to make a distasteful choice in order to avoid having an even worse outcome forced upon him. In 1973, the region was awash in union proposals as governments used the language of pan-Arabism to build alliances and balance against perceived threats. While Bourguiba might have preferred to remain above the fray, he may have determined that there simply was no way for Tunisia to avoid being drawn into some kind of union or federation with one of its larger neighbors. Additionally, Bourguiba faced mounting opposition at home. Ties to Libya could generate important economic benefits. Qadhafi was charismatic and popular, but he was also young, naïve, and—perhaps—manageable. After his rejection by the Egyptians, he would feel intense pressure to legitimize his pan-Arab message by making some kind of union with someone. He would likely turn to his easiest and closest target—Tunisia. If Tunisia resisted, Qadhafi might use force. Better to be proactive. Better to draw Qadhafi into an arrangement that would placate him, give Tunisia some authority, and buy time until Bourguiba could extricate himself from the deal.

These various explanations are not mutually exclusive. Reality may have involved elements of several of them. Regardless of the precise causes, the Arab Islamic Union was short-lived. Several of Bourguiba's most trusted advisors, particularly Prime Minister Hedi Nouira, objected vehemently to the deal. Given Bourguiba's health, putting the armed services under Qadhafi was tantamount to surrender. The US and France also expressed grave concerns about the union. Closer to home, Algeria saw the union as a threat to regional stability. There were even rumors that the Algerians moved troops into the border region to increase the pressure on Bourguiba (Chneguir 2004: 178). Weighed down by these pressures, and by questions about the treaty's legal status in Tunisia, the union fell apart in less than a month.

Relations between Tunisia and Libya deteriorated rapidly after the union collapsed. Unable to dominate Tunisia, Qadhafi began working to topple Bourguiba by exploiting the tensions inside Tunisia. In March 1976, Tunisian officials arrested a group of Libyans who had plotted the assassinations of Tunisia's prime and foreign ministers. Libya responded by expelling 1,800 Tunisian workers and by launching a virulent anti-Tunisian press campaign. The expulsions deprived Tunisia of those workers' remittances and added to the country's unemployment problem. Some believe that Libya also encouraged the Tunisian labor union to launch the January, 1978 general strike that degenerated into bloody clashes between marchers and security forces (ibid.: 181–2).

Qadhafi's brashest attempt to subvert the Tunisian government came two years later. On the night of January 26–27, 1980, a force of approximately 60 commandos attacked Tunisian security forces in the town of Gafsa. The commandos were Tunisians who had received training and logistical support from an organization based in Tripoli called the Revolutionary Movement for the Liberation of Tunisia. They had built arms caches around the city, hoping that their initial attack would spark a popular uprising and spread across the country. Security forces succeeded in retaking the town by the end of the following day, but the attack underscored the importance of thwarting connections between domestic organizations and foreign actors.

Relations between Tunisia and Libya remained strained through the 1980s. Libya expelled another 30,000 Tunisian workers in 1985. Like the previous round, these expulsions, and the strict remittance controls placed on remaining Tunisian workers in Libya, deprived Tunisia of an important income stream at a time of deepening economic crisis. But these tensions did help to solidify French and US support for Bourguiba. Both countries provided military assistance to Tunisia during the Gafsa crisis. In its wake, they helped Tunisia modernize its military and security forces. France, in particular, became an important source of loans to help Tunisia cope with the reduced flow of worker remittances from Libya in the 1980s.

After Ben Ali came to power, improving relations across the Maghreb and building an organization to facilitate regional cooperation became important themes in his foreign policy. They were not new themes. In the early 1960s Bourguiba concluded that the success of Tunisia's industrialization effort depended on having access to a larger regional market (Chneguir 2004: 116). He pressed Algeria and Morocco for integrated development plans, coordinated positions in trade talks with Europe, and other concrete measures that would create meaningful connective tissue between the three economies. In March 1965, Tunisia hosted the first meeting of a new Permanent Consultative Commission. This commission took on the tasks of conducting studies and organizing subcommittees that would develop cooperative strategies for specific economic sectors. Libya soon joined and the governments agreed to create a new Center for Industrial Studies in Tripoli.

Very quickly, however, it became clear that Maghrebi governments lacked the will to follow through with these plans. These were young governments, eager to develop their own economies. None wanted to sign any agreement that made its development dependent on the goodwill of its neighbors. Algeria, in particular, had no real interest in integrated development schemes. Its hydrocarbon wealth allowed it to pursue its own industrialization program without help from anyone else in the region. Tensions from the independence struggles, border disputes, and fundamental philosophical differences combined with economic self-interest to stymie meaningful progress towards economic cooperation. Nothing ever came of the Permanent Commission's plans and Algeria and Libya soon pulled out of it. The Commission continued to exist, but the region's governments still negotiated agreements and treaties on a bilateral basis. The notion of Maghrebi economic integration went nowhere for the next twenty years.

By the late 1980s, domestic economic crises across the region and the challenges posed by European integration created a stronger interest in cooperation. For all of the region's economies, growth depended on expanded trade and private investment. Economic integration would create a larger market, make the Maghreb more attractive to outside investors, and enhance North African bargaining power with Europe. In Algiers, at the June 1988 Arab League Summit, Tunisia, Algeria, Morocco, Mauritania, and Libya formed a new Grand Commission to develop specific measures that would facilitate greater union. In Marrakech, the following February, the five heads of state signed an agreement creating the Arab Maghreb Union (UMA).

Tunisia has been the UMA's strongest supporter. Ben Ali is "the conscience of the Maghreb" and the only head of state to attend every UMA summit (Mortimer 1999: 182, 189). By agreement of the member states, a Tunisian serves as the UMA's secretary-general at the headquarters in Rabat. The organization helped to improve Tunisian-Libyan relations in the late 1990s and helped to end Libya's diplomatic isolation. Ben Ali worked hard to get Qadhafi to join the new organization. The two countries reopened their borders to goods and people. Libya unfroze Tunisian assets. The two governments also resolved their long-standing dispute over the Gulf of Gabes (Chneguir 2004: 226). In 2003, the two governments negotiated a free trade agreement that helped Libya become Tunisia's number one Arab trading partner and a major source of tourism dollars.

The broader picture has been much less encouraging. Twenty years after its founding, the UMA lies dormant. The list of delays and outright failures is long. Several governments are behind in paying their contributions to the UMA's meager budget. The commitments to creating a free-exchange zone and to allowing the free movement of people and goods remain unfulfilled. As a result, inter-Maghreb trade still accounts for only 3.5 percent of the region's total trade. Beyond the secretary-general's office, none of the UMA's permanent institutions functions with any regularity. Most significantly, the UMA's Supreme Council, made up of the five heads of state, has not met since 1994. The current secretary-general, an experienced Tunisian diplomat named Habib Ben Yahia, proposed reforms to enhance the organization's ability to act in a memorandum to the foreign ministers in 2005. Four years later, none of them have responded (Ghorbal 2009).

The stumbling block is politics. Despite the rhetoric about economic integration, "[t]he impetus that produced the UMA in 1989 had much more to do with diplomacy than economic cooperation" (Mortimer 1999: 184). In 1988, Morocco accepted a United Nations plan to conduct a referendum on the future of the Western Sahara. That breakthrough, and the hope that a regional organization could forge a final solution to the conflict and maintain a regional power balance, played as large a role in the UMA's founding as any belief in the benefits of economic integration. The lack of progress on the Sahara issue, and worsening relations between Algeria and Morocco (the border between the two countries closed in the mid-1990s), have prevented any meaningful development of the UMA. Civil war in Algeria, concerns about Islamism spilling across borders, and Libya's frustration with its UMA "brothers" for not providing more support during the conflict with the international community over the Lockerbie bombings have all created additional obstacles to regional cooperation.

A 1963 assessment of the prospects for Maghrebi unity concluded that:

> While unity is sought in principle, little is done for its practical implementation. Unity threatens to cost more in the independence of the individual countries from each other than it is certain to contribute to the reduction of continuing dependence on the ex- and neo-colonial powers.
>
> (Liska 1963: 1)

This analysis rings as true today as it did then. It likely will continue to do so. Because the economic ties between the Maghrebi states remain so weak, "the UMA depends even more than other regional economic schemes on the political will of the partners to place a very high priority upon regional cooperation" (Mortimer 1999: 178). Unless the region's governments resolve their differences or reform the UMA in ways that allow it to function in spite of them, each government will continue its own quest for markets, investors, and security. There is no reason to believe that either of these changes will come about anytime soon. Tunisia's stability, openness, and educated population will allow it to compete well compared to most of its neighbors. But the region as a whole will continue to miss the benefits— political and economic, domestic and regional—of greater cooperation and stability.

5 Stability, reform, and Tunisia's future

Tunisians take great and justifiable pride in their country's accomplishments over the past five decades. Compared to other Arab and African countries, especially non-OPEC countries, Tunisia boasts one of the developing world's most impressive human development records. There are richer countries. There are more democratic countries. But across a broad range of outcomes—economic growth, distribution of wealth, education, health care, gender equity, absence of violent domestic or international conflict—Tunisia's record faces scant competition.

Tunisia's stability and pragmatic leadership account for much of this success. As the chapters in this book demonstrate, stability and pragmatism characterize the country at two levels. At the most general level, Tunisia's basic political and economic order has never experienced a violent or revolutionary transformation that redistributed political and economic power in a fundamental way. Reform, not revolution, was the core demand of Tunisian nationalists from the Young Tunisians through the Neo-Destour. The transition to independence involved relatively little disturbance to the process of state formation underway since the late Ottoman period. Stability also characterizes Tunisia's approach to the specific issues addressed here. In terms of domestic politics, economic policy, and foreign relations, core interests and the basic strategies for serving those interests have changed relatively little. Ideology has exerted very little influence in Tunisia's public life. Pragmatism, not orthodoxy, has provided the guiding light. This was the essence of "Bourguibism". It has continued under Ben Ali.

Some root Tunisia's stability and pragmatism in a distinct Tunisian personality. The absence of violent conflict and the country's close political, economic, and cultural ties to Europe have generated a political culture that shuns violence and emphasizes rationalism, negotiation, and rule-making under the direction of a strong central state. This culture generates a shared allergy to violence and revolutionary change.

These historical and cultural considerations are important. Tunisia's relative secularism and its progressive social legislation, particularly on issues of gender, clearly reflect the philosophical influence of its ties to France and Europe. But these traditions cannot, by themselves, explain Tunisia's persistent stability. Other countries with similar attributes have experienced very different trajectories. Substantial elements of Tunisia's own political life do not fit well with a tradition that emphasizes competition between ideas and rule-governed behavior for all.

This book has argued that two broad sets of factors account for Tunisia's stability. The first involves some basic, objective circumstances that shape the country's existence: its small size, its location, its narrow resource base. These factors do not determine policies or outcomes in Tunisia. But they do set real constraints on what Tunisia's policymakers can do. This is particularly true for economic and foreign policies. Our discussions of both issues emphasized the great stability that has characterized Tunisia's goals. In economic terms, Tunisia has steadily pursued a form of state capitalism that pursues growth through private sector activity and, increasingly, through involvement in the global economy. The rhetoric and the specific points of emphasis have varied in response to more immediate political needs, but Tunisia's fundamental approach to economic development has changed very little since independence. Change in economic policy has tended to move in the direction of greater fidelity to its core approach rather than away from it. Tunisia's small domestic market, its small domestic entrepreneurial class, and the absence of abundant, high-value export commodities give it little opportunity to pursue any other kind of development strategy.

Likewise, Tunisian foreign policymakers work with a relatively small tool kit. Tunisia is a small country with two much larger, oil-rich neighbors who have developed very different domestic political systems and foreign policies that have, at times, threatened Tunisia's sovereignty. Maintaining independence without incurring the economic costs and political risks of a large military has been Tunisia's steady goal. The needs to secure strong protectors, to avoid costly military conflict, and to encourage European investment, create strong incentives for Tunisia to pursue a policy that emphasizes regional cooperation, negotiated conflict resolution, and strong relations with France and the United States. Particularly in light of shared concerns about Islamist violence and shared commitments to markets and trade, there is no reason to believe that the fundamentals of Tunisia's foreign policy will change anytime soon.

The second set of factors that explain Tunisia's stability involve governing strategies that successfully combine authoritarian control with sustained investment in social development. This combination traces its roots to the independence struggle, but its contours have changed over time. Bourguiba and Ben Ali came to the presidency under different circumstances, and each brought different assets to the job.

Two Presidencies: Two Authoritarianisms

Bourguiba's authoritarianism developed from the unique conditions that existed at independence. The Neo-Destour thoroughly dominated the political and organizational landscape. It enjoyed broad and deep support as the organization that led the country to independence and as a dispenser of patronage. It maintained a strong national structure that reached into every corner of the country and into every professional or social organization. This dominance gave Tunisia a strong, national structure that could take charge of the whole country. But it also deprived the country of any political or ideological counterweight.

Bourguiba also entered post-independence politics with tremendous personal support for his role as the architect of Tunisia's struggle against France. His charismatic style and his shrewd strategizing had established a coalition of support within the party that bolstered his own position and undermined his competitors. As much as he believed in the Neo-Destour, however, he remained fiercely dedicated to his own freedom to maneuver as he saw fit. He believed that he alone possessed the wisdom and vision to lead the country. He would not allow anyone or any organization—including the party he built—to limit his ability to follow his own pragmatic counsel.

Despite his strength, Bourguiba did face challenges. He still had to contend with serious opposition from the Youssefists who rejected his Western orientation and his strategy of negotiating independence in stages. He also felt pressure from Tunisia's small communist party and his allies in the labor movement. Their support had been critical to his ascendency, but their pressure for a socialist development strategy threatened Bourguiba's independence and his support among more conservative elements of the party.

The desire to eliminate these threats and to protect his freedom prompted Bourguiba to become increasingly authoritarian in the decade following independence. Between the late 1950s and the mid-1970s, Tunisia developed the trappings of a corporatist system. It had unions for workers, students, farmers, business owners. The government protected these organizations' monopolies over their members and consulted them on matters related to their interests.

In reality, however, Tunisia did not develop the actual substance of a corporatist system. The Neo-Destour/PSD became indistinguishable from the state and it worked to dominate all forms of professional and associational life. The party/state bureaucracy wanted unions and other corporatist organizations to implement its policies, not to represent their members' interests in a more independent way. Moreover, there was no real bargaining process. Bourguiba established himself as the maker and breaker of careers in a highly personalized style that converted policy management into people management. The *combattant suprême* became the *arbitre suprême*. As Bourguiba himself admitted in response to a question in the early 1960s about the nature of Tunisia's political system: "The system? What system? I am the system".[1] "Alive or dead", he told another reporter during the same period, "I am responsible for this nation's destiny".[2]

This method protected Bourguiba's freedom to maneuver and allowed him to pursue policies for which he received extensive praise in Europe and the US—progressive, secular social legislation; a decidedly pro-Western foreign policy that rejected communism and pan-Arabism. But this method also left the country without sufficient institutions for checking presidential power, for expressing and reconciling competing interests, or for transferring presidential power from one person to another. Too much of the country's business was conducted through Bourguiba's manipulation of a handful of key individuals. Complex issues took on the added dynamics of personal rivalries.

This highly personalized style, and Bourguiba's sense that no one else could replace him, limited his willingness to use reform to relieve mounting tensions in the 1970s and 1980s. He could have crafted reforms that addressed the most pressing issues of the day: the presidential succession, the relationship between the ruling party and the state, demands for liberalization within the ruling party, the role of other parties and movements. He could have designed these measures in ways that responded to rising pressures for reform while protecting, even enhancing, his power. But he did not, in part because these reforms might have reduced his room for maneuver and his ability to rule by manipulating all other political players.

There are two elements of irony in this. Bourguiba understood, intellectually, that institutions make an important contribution to stability. In a conversation about the transition to independent government, he declared that, "When there are no institutions, there is chaos".[3] But his sense of his own importance prevented him from acting on this insight.

More importantly, preemptive reform only works if rulers act while they still enjoy considerable power. They must have the foresight to recognize early signs of crumbling before the ground gives way beneath them. Throughout much of his career, Bourguiba demonstrated precisely this kind of prescience. He had a keen ability to cut away rhetoric and romanticism and to see outcomes that others could not or would not see. From the mid-1970s on, however, Bourguiba seemed progressively unable or unwilling to be the wily, pragmatic strategist he had been during the independence struggle and the early years of his presidency. By the time conditions had become grave enough to prompt serious discussions of reform, he had lost the ability to be a successful preemptive reformer. His stature and the PSD's had slipped so far that Bourguiba and others in the party feared that reform would simply allow the opposition to finish them off. Because stability and reform could not work together in the highly personalized system that Bourguiba built, his last decade in power became the most serious period of instability in the country's post-independence history.

Ben Ali stepped onto a very different national stage as a very different kind of national savior. In sharp contrast to the broad support that Bourguiba and the Neo-Destour enjoyed at independence, Ben Ali inherited a government and a ruling party that had lost much of their credibility. That government also faced a well-organized Islamist organization with strong support in urban areas. The economy remained very fragile, and the government had accepted a structural adjustment plan that would involve difficult reforms. Ben Ali stepped onto this stage without a reputation for charismatic national leadership or the influential relationships of a long-time party boss.

He did benefit, however, from critical assets that shaped the way he would govern. First, most Tunisians were simply relieved to see someone step in, remove Bourguiba, and pull the country back from the brink of serious unrest. Second, although the PSD had lost a great deal of credibility, it had not lost its ability to govern the country effectively. Ben Ali's coup did not constitute a fundamental rupture with the old order, so he did not have to build a new one. Just as Bourguiba and the Neo-Destour had stepped into the governing institutions established under the French Protectorate, Ben Ali could make use of the same institutions that had developed over the previous three decades. He simply had to revitalize them and restore public confidence in them. Finally, he brought an intimate knowledge of the country's security apparatus.

With these tools, Ben Ali built a system that is very centralized, but much less personalized than Bourguiba's. While Bourguiba constructed a state corporatist façade over a highly personalized management style, Ben Ali constructed a liberal democratic façade over a centralized and insulated technocracy. The new president quickly snatched away most of the secular opposition's long-standing demands with rhetoric that emphasized human rights, individual liberty, and political competition. He made it easier for new parties to form, to run in elections, and to win seats. He even has allowed other candidates to run for the presidency. Tunisia today has eight legal political parties besides the ruling RCD. It has the oldest human rights league in the Arab world. It has professional associations or unions for workers, women, journalists, lawyers, and students. The government at least tolerates the existence of several newspapers, magazines, and civil society organizations, many of which have explicitly political programs. Most of these organizations, particularly the parties, have been established since Ben Ali came to power. There is no denying that his reforms have created formal space for public discourse and engagement that did not exist under Bourguiba.

But Ben Ali carefully crafted these reforms in ways that set very real limits on the amount of actual power that the opposition can win at the ballot box and the amount of criticism they can level through the media or human rights organizations. Electoral rules divide the opposition parties against each other and make it impossible for any of them to win a majority. They also make it impossible for any candidate besides Ben Ali to win the presidency. Most importantly, this arrangement allows Ben Ali and the RCD to control the pace and content of reforms.[4] These tactics, along with more visibly aggressive forms of repression, have forced the opposition to focus on legalistic issues that generate little public enthusiasm.

While authoritarianism has been the defining characteristic of Tunisia's politics, it is important to note that both presidents have leavened it with steady investment in human development. Since the 1960s, Tunisia has been a leader in family planning, education, health care, electrification, and water supply. Since the late 1980s, Ben Ali has taken great care to package and pace economic reforms in ways that minimize social disruption.

For both presidents, this attention to social development reflects an honest commitment to improving the quality of life for Tunisians. But it also consti-tutes an investment in the stability that is vital to a small, resource-poor country whose economic development depends on engagement with the global economy. Both Bourguiba and Ben Ali have valued domestic stability as a vital tool in their efforts to deter meddling by larger neighbors, to reduce the need for an expensive (and potentially troublesome) military, and to attract external financial and political support.

The same is true for a wide range of interests in the country. Given the objective conditions that shape Tunisia's life, stability is prerequisite to almost everything for almost everyone. Down the length of Tunisia's modern history, there have been very few interests for whom the benefits of serious unrest outweighed its costs. This is partly a function of the government's success at drawing critical interests into the party's and the government's patronage networks. But it also reflects the widespread belief that domestic unrest in such a small, exposed country would undermine the economy and a quality of life that most Tunisians know is the highest in the region. Both presidents have understood this well. They have dangled the prospect of unrest spinning out of control to encourage opponents to limit what they will do for the sake of change. This has been particularly true of Ben Ali, who has pointed to Algeria's experience in the 1990s as evidence of what can happen when governments legalize Islamist parties and liberalize their politics too quickly.

Prospects for Democracy

The result, then, is an authoritarianism that enjoys at least the grudging support of a majority of the population. It also stands in sharp contrast to what many expected of Tunisia in the middle and late 1980s. As we have discussed, Tunisia seemed to have so many of the socio-economic pre-requisites for democratic government. Ben Ali's democratic rhetoric and his weak connection to the ruling party reinforced the perception that Tunisia was ready to move beyond Bourguiba's nation-building authoritarianism. The global context at the time also shaped expectations about what would happen in an authoritarian system facing a serious legitimacy crisis. The late

1980s and 1990s saw popular movements replace worn-out authoritarian orders with new democratic ones in several regions. Talk of globalization, the end of grand ideological conflicts, and the inevitable spread of market economies and democratic politics dominated much of the scholarly and public discourse.[5]

In this environment, it was easy to believe that Tunisia was ripe for a democratic transition. By 1987, Bourguiba personified the kind of tired, inept authoritarianism whose time had passed. His erratic management of the Islamist opposition—and of his own government—had created a serious crisis that threatened the very stability he had worked hard to maintain for three decades. If the authoritarian order was cracking, what could replace it in the late 1980s and early 1990s but democracy?

We now appreciate more keenly that transitions from authoritarian rule are fragile and contingent things. Roughly two decades' worth of scholarship has shown how easy and common it is for even weakened authoritarians to divide and conquer their opponents through a combination of repression and strategic reform.[6] It is clearer now than it was in the late 1980s and early 1990s that the deck was stacked heavily against democracy in Tunisia. First, there was no coherent, united democratic opposition movement. Islamists and a variety of secular democrats agreed that Bourguiba needed to go. But there was no single organization that brought these fractious elements together behind a set of common principles and a reasonably coherent strategy in the way that the Neo-Destour built the independence movement in the forties and 1950s. *Movements* can generate lots of demonstrators. But they rarely produce new governments by themselves. They need *organizations*.

They also benefit from allies, powerful individuals inside the authoritarian government who conclude that the balance of power has shifted and that the government likely will fall. In many cases, those individuals see the pragmatic wisdom in building bridges to the people who they believe will soon rule. Their cooperation enhances the opposition's strength and facilitates a smoother transition.

Even if Tunisia had developed a more effective pro-democracy organization in the early 1990s, that movement would have attracted few elite allies. Powerful individuals at the top of the government had also concluded that Bourguiba had to go. But they had not concluded that Tunisia needed a fundamentally different kind of government. If Bourguiba's power had been greatly diminished when Ben Ali replaced him, the state's had not. Its ability to reward supporters and punish opponents remained very much intact. Once Ben Ali had taken over, there was no reason for any calculating high-level official to conclude that the balance of power in Tunisia had shifted enough to make it wise to work with the democratic opposition. As the chapter on politics makes clear, this continues to be the case today.

This brings us to the central trade-off in Tunisian public life. Tunisia's political system does combine stability and reform. But the mix strongly favors the status quo. It is the government that shapes the content and pace of reform; it does so with a strong preference for as little change as possible. One the one hand, this centralized authority has allowed the government to take bold actions that it might not have taken if it had been more constrained by public opinion or by legislative or bureaucratic haggling. A less authoritarian government might not have adopted such a progressive Personal Status Code, called such a rapid halt to failing economic policies in the late 1960s, or adopted the unpopular economic measures in the late 1980s and early 1990s that laid the foundation for subsequent growth. This is the mix of stability and reform that positions Tunisia well for the challenges and opportunities that will come with deeper integration into the global economy. This is the Tunisia that combines a stable investment climate and prudent macro-economic policies with a strong, pragmatic executive who has the freedom to shape policy in response to rapidly changing economic conditions.

But this is also the Tunisia that has yet to change presidents at the ballot box. In fact, Tunisians today face many of the same fundamental questions and dilemmas that have dominated their political life for most of the post-independence period: How much political competition can their country tolerate without undermining stability? How can they establish stronger processes for checking presidential power, including processes that subject the presidency to meaningful electoral competition, and for protecting individual expression? How can Tunisia have an opposition that is both meaningful and loyal? What is Islam's place in the political process? Do Tunisians want a political system with a different mix of stability and reform, a mix that creates more meaningful competition for power, but that also generates greater uncertainty about policy-making?

This book does not presume to tell Tunisians how they should answer these questions. They enjoy a quality of life that stands as compelling evidence in favor of a cautious approach to political change. As we noted at the end of the chapter on Tunisia's economy, however, there is also a compelling argument that suggests that the status quo will not be able to sustain this quality of life in the midst of a rapidly changing economic environment. The changes necessary to meet those challenges go beyond technocratic policy engineering. They will involve more dramatic political changes that create more room for individual choice and public competition on a range of issues. If uncertainty is the defining characteristic of the contemporary economy, uncertainty—bounded by rules—may also be the defining characteristic of the political system that is best able to succeed over the long term. If this is true, what kinds of changes would be necessary in order to generate more substantial change?

Because we tend to think of democracy first in terms of elections, the most obvious answers to this question start there. It is certainly true that Tunisia's electoral rules must change so that opposition parties have opportunities not only to win seats, but to win enough of them to govern. In order for that to happen, opposition parties, the media, and civil society organizations must have more freedom to organize, to govern themselves, and to criticize the government without inviting meddling or repression. The government must also be willing to accept the verdict of the ballot box.

These changes are vital and many people inside and out of Tunisia have demanded them. But making these changes durable depends on deeper, less obvious changes. Basic rights and liberties are secure only when they reflect more than the position of the current president or governing party. If they reflect no more than that, then they are subject to easy change when the president changes, when the governing party changes, or when either simply changes its mind. To be meaningful, basic rights and liberties must be articulated clearly in a constitution that is truly foundational. It must have a legal status that goes beyond a mere legislative act so that it cannot be altered easily by legislative act. Tunisia's constitution does not currently enjoy this status. The ease with which the National Assembly has passed laws that restrict freedoms of assembly and expression, and the ease with which it has extended two presidents' terms of office, illustrate the dangers.

One could argue that these are the predictable excesses of single-party rule. The solution is to change the electoral laws and vote a variety of parties into parliament. The diversity will create a competitive marketplace of ideas that makes majorities harder for form, ensures that only legislation with broad support gets passed, and provides a check against anti-democratic legislation. From this Madisonian perspective, everyone will share a vested interest in sustaining institutions—rather than individuals—because the institutions give everyone a right to play and a fair opportunity to compete and win. Today's electoral losers remain loyal to the system because the rules offer a fair chance of winning next time.

Making it difficult to form majorities can be a good thing for democracy, but it can be a tough sell in countries where even democrats fear gridlock that prevents their government from acting quickly and decisively on critical issues. More importantly, having a multi-party parliament does not address the basic point. Such a parliament might be more committed to democratic rights and liberties. But unless the constitution that guarantees these rights enjoys independent heft, unless the courts are free to judge all laws—and all citizens—in light of that constitution, then rights and liberties remain subject to presidential or parliamentary whim. In sum, democracy will only succeed if there is a constitutional order that lays out the basic parameters within which all citizens, including government officials, must play the game. As noted earlier, this is what it means to say that Tunisia must become a state of law rather than man or ruling party.

Attitudes about the meaning of "opposition" also have to change. We noted that Tunisian politics exhibits a strong majoritarian element that dates to the independence struggle. First as a nationalist movement and then as a single party, the Neo-Destour/PSD/RCD has claimed to provide a very large political tent for all Tunisians. Because the party represented everyone, and because all legitimate debate took place within its ranks, its decisions necessarily reflected the will of "the people" or "the nation". To oppose the party's decisions was to oppose that expressed will. Since the party claimed to make room for everyone, there was no reason—except for rank ambition—to form another party. This environment left no room for the idea of "loyal opposition". Opposing the party, or criticizing it in ways that went beyond the very constrained bounds of its own debate, became an act of treason.

Beyond an intolerance of multiple parties, this majoritarian view contributed to the longstanding ambiguity about the relationship between the government and civil society organizations and the press. It has been difficult for these organizations to act as representatives of particular interests, as critics, or as independent sources of reflection and policy recommendation. This lack of independence stems in part from the fact that many of these organizations were established by the ruling party or relied heavily on it for funds and leadership. But the intolerance of minority opinion within the party and state bureaucracies has exacerbated the ambiguity surrounding their role. Party and government leaders may allow these organizations to represent their constituents within the narrow parameters of debate within the party. But once a policy decision has been made, party and state leaders expect these organizations to become obedient executors of that decision. Again, public dissent and opposition becomes "undemocratic" because they reflect an unwillingness to support the will of the majority.

It is important to note that this majoritarian view of democracy does not only shape politics within the ruling party or between the ruling party and other parties and organizations. It also shapes politics within opposition parties and civil society organizations. These organizations often betray the same intolerance of minority opinion within their own ranks. This intolerance weakens opposition organizations in several ways. Because opposition to the majority is perceived as something akin to treason, differences of opinion within the organization turn into debilitating personal conflicts. Organizations break down into competing factions headed by leaders who denounce one another as corrupt and anti-democratic. Most of Tunisia's opposition parties have suffered from this dynamic. Their own internal fractiousness makes it easier for the government to divide and conquer these organizations and to prevent them from forming a unified opposition front. It also undermines the oppositions' credibility with the general public. It reinforces the impression that opposition organizations are little more than cliques of petty, ambitious elites. Giving opposition parties more honest chances to win elections accounts for little if no one will vote for them.

This brings us to another challenge facing democratic politics in Tunisia: apathy. Tunisia has become a very apolitical place over the past two decades. The vast majority of the population, and particularly of the middle class that many hold up as the engine of democratic change, has simply opted out of politics. Large numbers believe that the government is corrupt. They find its authoritarianism repugnant and embarrassing. But they also recognize that the government has provided a degree of stability and prosperity that is unequalled in the region. Just as important, they do not see a meaningful alternative. The ruling party and the exceptionally strong presidency have monopolized the political process so thoroughly that no other party or individual has been able to develop into a compelling candidate for control of the government. Even if the rules were fairer, the opposition parties seem to be self-interested parlor societies that do not model good democratic behavior within their own ranks. In this environment, political engagement involves a choice between two options: join the RCD and participate in a system that many find deeply objectionable, or join an opposition organization—a choice that offers little chance of having a meaningful impact but a real chance of running afoul of the regime. Faced with that choice, most Tunisians make no choice at all. This large-scale abstention from politics makes it very difficult for opposition organizations to muster the following they need in order to press for reforms that give them a meaningful chance of winning.

One other issue hovers at the edges of the debates about democracy, rights, and liberties: the role of Islam in public life. The government's crackdown on Ennahdha stifled debate about this question more than it resolved it. Islam has a long association with political opposition in modern Tunisia. Bourguiba's primary rival during the nationalist struggle and the early years after independence emphasized traditional Islamic and pan-Arab values. In the early 1980s, Islamist organizations emerged again as the most powerful opposition to Bourguiba and then to Ben Ali. Even during periods when there was no active Islamist opposition, religion has been a source of latent tension between a predominantly secular ruling elite and a general population that has been relatively more conservative and religious.[7]

This history complicates the conversation about Islam's place in the public sphere. "Islam" enters that conversation with a reputation as a threat to the status quo rather than as a component of the culture that shapes the identities and values of many citizens. The fact that the law currently prohibits parties with religious references in their names provides evidence of this basic association of "Islam" with "opposition". This is not to suggest that most Tunisians want to legalize Islamist parties or that they should want to do so. But neither is there good reason to believe that all Tunisians want to exclude all forms of political belief, expression, or action that makes explicit reference to Islam or that draws inspiration from the faith in some way. The point here is simply to say that Islam's place in Tunisia's public life remains unresolved, and the only durable resolution is one that reflects preferences beyond the government's.

It would take a long time to make these changes in Tunisia. Since the early 1990s, it has been common to hear Tunisians and others suggest that change will become more likely if the economy deteriorates. Indeed, several opposition politicians in the early and mid-1990s suggested that they were simply biding their time. They argued that Tunisia's stability rested on two shaky foundations that would eventually collapse: fear of an Islamist takeover and conjunctural economic prosperity. The first would give way steadily as it became clear that Islamists pose no serious threat in Tunisia. The second would collapse when the economy experienced a downturn that generated material grievances across a broad cross-section of the population. They argued that Tunisia's economic success in the 1990s was the product of good weather and good luck, factors beyond the government's control. Once the conjuncture shifted, the economy would decline and people would become less willing to tolerate Ben Ali's authoritarianism and more willing to support opposition movements.

This is not a sound strategy for building a healthy democracy in Tunisia because it is not a strategy at all. The protests against Ben Salah's collectivization program in the late 1960s, the broad opposition that developed around the UGTT in the mid-1970s, and the rising popularity of the Islamists in the mid- and late 1980s demonstrate that periods of broad popular dissent in Tunisia have coincided with downturns in the economy. It is also true that economic grievances could make more Tunisians receptive to an opposition alternative. But there has to be a real alternative first. In the absence of an opposition party or a coalition of parties that is well-organized and that offers a credible and compelling program, popular unrest will only allow the regime to lash itself more firmly into power through a combination of repression and strategically crafted reforms. This is one of the lessons of Tunisia's experience in the 1970s and 1980s. Rising popular anger over economic hardship might generate unrest. But this is the kind of opposition that the government has proven able and willing to successfully repress.

Building the kind of opposition that could produce more substantive change will require time and some courageous risk-taking. It will require risk-taking not by desperate people who have nothing to lose, but by people who may, in fact, have a good deal to lose. The real agents of change in Tunisia will come from two populations. The first is the group of intellectuals and democratic and human rights advocates who traditionally have led and spoken for Tunisia's opposition. They have not always done this effectively. But they have valuable experience building organizations, formulating a message, and navigating Tunisia's authoritarian labyrinth.

The second, and arguably the more important, is the diverse group of individuals who have built businesses and prospered in recent years, but who have not been important enough for the regime to coopt through special favors and opportunities. The prospects for democratic change will improve considerably if and when these people find themselves unable to continue to prosper in an increasingly competitive economy unless they have more influence over the policymaking process. If that realization develops across enough members of this population; if it leads to discussions within that population about how a more open, competitive state of law can serve their interests; if those discussions lead to the formulation of a credible and compelling platform and to overtures to other democratic activists; if that platform finds a charismatic spokesperson who can turn out voters; if this movement can find allies inside the ruling elite who help them convince the president that he serves his own interests better by making substantial concessions rather than by cracking down, then the chance for systemic change will improve.

This is a long, incomplete, and perhaps improbable list of "ifs". One could craft a number of scenarios in which this process starts and then stalls at some point short of a truly competitive democratic system that respects individual and collective rights and liberties. But it is important to point out that a process like this is more likely to develop in an economy that is thriving through export-driven growth, not an economy marked by serious decline. This is so for at least three reasons. First, an economy that is growing through investment and deeper regional integration will generate more members of this critical population, members whose diverse economic activities and global linkages give them a stronger interest in influencing policy and make it more difficult for the state to coopt and control them. Second, as Tunisia's stability becomes more directly linked to the success of this kind of economy, the president will have stronger incentives to care about the preferences of these economic interests that are becoming more difficult to coopt and control. Third, stable economic growth will be critical to getting more Tunisians to vote for an alternative party and president. Casting this vote involves a step into economic, as well as political, uncertainty. The RCD, Ben Ali, and the state bureaucracy they control have decades of experience managing Tunisia's economy. Voting for an alternative means voting for people who have much less. If voters believe that economic growth—and their own welfare—remains tenuous, they will be inclined to vote for experience. But if they believe that the economy is structurally sound and that their own welfare is robust enough to withstand the fluctuation that might come with a transition in power, they may feel that they can afford the risk and uncertainty that would come from turning the government and the economy over to new managers.

None of this is inevitable. The circumstances and the choices that would produce the changes discussed here may not come together. Authoritarianism in Tunisia could prove to be very durable, and not simply because the government represses opponents. A majority of Tunisians may determine that the benefits of the status quo outweigh the individual and collective costs that a transition would require them to pay. In fact, the country's history and its current balance of political forces make this the safer bet over the medium term. It does seem clear, though, that political change in Tunisia will not come about through some dramatic event that suddenly replaces the existing order with a new one. The stability–reform dialectic that has driven Tunisian politics for the past five decades will continue to do so. The central question is whether or not that dialectic and the outcomes that it produces can be shaped in meaningful ways by more than one man and one party.

Notes

Introduction

1 "Al-Maghreb" is the Arabic term for "the West". "Al-Mashreq" refers to "the East". Definitions of the Maghreb's borders vary. When asked where the Mashreq ends and the Maghreb begins, Tunisia's first president, Habib Bourguiba, is reported to have replied, "at the line where people stop eating rice and start eating couscous". Today, the Maghreb refers to all of the Arabic-speaking countries west of Egypt: Libya, Tunisia, Algeria, Morocco, and Mauritania. These are the countries that make up the Arab Maghreb Union (UMA). Historically, however, the Maghreb has been most closely associated with the three countries that compose the heart of the region—Tunisia, Algeria, and Morocco.

1 State-Building and Independence in Tunisia

1 This version of Bourguiba and Sfar's first campaign stop in Ksar Hellal is based on Bourguiba's own account, given at a conference on the history of the nationalist movement. It is recounted in Kraiem (1996: 211–12).

2 For a richer discussion of Tunisia's pre-Ottoman history, including the Hafsid period, the Ottoman-Spanish competition, and the rise of the beylical office, see Abun Nasr (1987).

3 According to Moore (1965: 12), the bey ruled the countryside through approximately 60 caids and some 2,000 subordinate sheikhs.

4 For more detailed discussions of France's occupation of Algeria, see Abun Nasr (1987: 248–72) and Bennoune (1988: 29–59).

5 Mohammed Bey reigned for only four years. He succeeded Ahmed Bey in 1855 and served until his death in 1859.

6 The 1864 revolt is frequently described as a tribal affair. That it was. But it also involved the towns of the Sahel. Prior to 1863, the residents of Tunis, Sousse, Sfax, Monastir, and Kairouan had been exempt from the poll tax. In addition to doubling the tax, the government applied the new levy to them, as well.

7 For overviews of nationalist movements in the Maghreb, see Al-Fassi (1954), Moore (1970), and Abun Nasr (1987).

8 In Arabic-speaking countries outside the Maghreb, *habous* is known as *waqf*.

9 In 1901, Tunisia's Italian population—71,000—was still nearly three times as large as its French population—24,000 (Abun Nasr 1987: 295). The fact that French colonists had to actually buy land helped to keep the total number small and meant that they tended to be wealthier than Tunisia's Italian population. The French dominated colonial agriculture and the administration; the Italians worked predominantly in manual and skilled labor positions.

10 For more detailed discussions of land tenure institutions and the changes that the

Protectorate made to them, see Anderson (1986: 42–7; 151–7), Lahmar (1994), and Sethom (1992).

11 Abun Nasr (1987: 357) contends that total French landholdings never took in more than about 700,000 hectares, or one-fifth of Tunisia's arable land. But because these tended to be the best farming lands, the displacement effect on Tunisia's rural population was considerable.

12 The demand to stop hiring Italian drivers came in the wake of a tragic accident in which a train, driven by an Italian driver, struck and killed a Tunisian child.

13 It is interesting to note that *Le Tunisien* first appeared in 1907 as a French-language paper. The Young Tunisians did not put out an Arabic-language version until 1909.

14 The Sahel was the region of Tunisia that remained least disrupted by the economic effects of the Protectorate. It was the region with the longest history of settled agriculture, practiced by individual farmers whose holdings remained intact. At a time when the working class had not yet developed sufficiently to act as a powerful force and traditional urban elites had been either coopted or broken by the Protectorate, this independent and stable economic base allowed the Sahel to become the region that dominated the nationalist movement as it developed over the course of the 1930s and 1940s (Salem 1984: 39).

2 Authoritarianism and Stability in Tunisian Politics

1 Youssefists controlled the Neo-Destour's powerful Tunis federation and made it difficult for Bourguiba to organize meetings and rally his forces in the capital city. Habib Achour, one of Bourguiba's long-time associates and the head of the UGTT's regional union in Sfax, promised to provide protection if Bourguiba would call a party congress in Sfax. The success of that congress and its support for Bourguiba fueled the conflict with the Youssefists and established the UGTT as a strong Bourguibist constituency within the party. See Achour (1989).

2 Bourguiba was shrewdly managing two issues by removing Ben Salah from the UGTT and giving him the Social Affairs position. He neutralized a potential political opponent but integrated him more deeply into the ruling system. This allowed Bourguiba to benefit from Ben Salah's talent, but put him clearly under Bourguiba's thumb. At the same time, Toumi (1989: 53) suggests that Bourguiba was sending a message to conservative elements who wanted to force him to pursue a liberal economic development strategy. By moving Ben Salah, but keeping him in the government, Bourguiba was telling them, "Alright, you get a liberal economic model. But beware. I didn't definitively eliminate your enemy; and remember that if I make you, I can break you".

3 In a letter that he left to Bourguiba after his death, Ahmed Tlili, who became the UGTT's General Secretary through this government intervention, admitted that he had allowed himself to become an "instrument of despotism" (Toumi 1989: 52).

4 Mestiri told *Le Figaro* that "the congress spoke clearly in our favor in terms of both ideas and of personnel. This happened in spite of the wide range of pressures brought to bear on the delegates. These methods included pure and simple intimidation by armed men from Ouardenine who stood outside the meeting place" (quoted in Azaiez 1983: 77).

5 Many believe that Ben Salah could not have escaped prison and fled the country without the assistance of supporters inside the government. When Ben Salah refused to endorse participation in elections in the early 1980s, some disillusioned members of the party broke away and established the *Parti de l'Unité Populaire* (PUP). The Tunisian government legalized the PUP in 1983.

6 For detailed discussions of the development of Tunisia's Islamist movement, see Burgat and Dowell (1993), Waltz (1986), Dunn (1994a), and Shahin (1997).

7 For more on the bread riots that broke out Tunisia and Morocco in January 1984, see Seddon (1984).

8 As Emma Murphy notes (1999: 164), the circumstances surrounding Ben Ali's coup became the subject of considerable discussion in Tunisia. However concerned Ben Ali was about an Islamist surge if the retrials began, many believe that he was also moved to action by the fear that Mohamed Sayah was preparing a coup of his own. Sayah occupied several high positions under Bourguiba, including Director of the PSD. Much of this speculation may have been fueled by the fact that security forces arrested Sayah very shortly after the coup. Even after he returned home, Sayah remained under close surveillance for several years.

9 For a detailed discussion of Ben Ali's early reforms, see Zartman (1991) and Murphy (1999: 164–92).

10 Mounting unrest in Algeria strengthened the Tunisian opposition's belief that self-interest would compel Ben Ali to make good on his democratic pledges. When large riots broke out in Algiers in October, 1988, Tunisian opposition leaders saw them as a reaction to decades of authoritarian, single-party rule. They believed that Ben Ali would make additional reforms once he secured his position in order to avoid a similar fate. See Belhassen (1988).

11 Ennahdha leaders contend that they had negotiated a deal with the secular parties, particularly the MDS. Islamist leaders knew that they did not have a coherent plan for running the country alone, and they knew that Tunisia's secular political and economic elite would never accept them as the ruling party. Without the cooperation of these elites, the Islamists would never be able to generate economic growth, administer the country and maintain broad popular support. Consequently, they agreed not to make their own bid for power and to work with the secular parties in support of a presidential candidate acceptable to the country's elite. In return, the secular parties would support Ennahdha's bid for legalization and would allow it to participate in the political process. This account of the relations between Tunisia's Islamist and secular opposition parties is based on the author's interview with Rachid al-Ghannouchi, President of Ennahdha, in London, January 13,1998.

12 This discussion of the single list controversy is based on Daoud (1990: 681–2) and on the author's January 13, 1998, interview with Rachid al-Ghannouchi.

13 See also Guitta (2007).

14 The reform added proportionality to the old constituency-based system by creating a dichotomy between the allocation of seats and the allocation of electoral districts. The code established one seat for every 52,500 Tunisians. But the new code established electoral districts on the basis of one deputy per 60,000 Tunisians. This dichotomy in the allocation of seats vs. districts created a parliament with 163 seats. Some 144 would be allocated according to the old system; the other 19 would be allocated proportionally across the parties that fielded lists in a district but did not win the majority. See Dunn (1994b).

15 Khemais Chemari, leader of the MDS, quoted in *La Croix*, March 19, 1994.

16 Manai (1995) and Beau and Tuquoi (1999) provide two book-length discussions of human rights abuses under Ben Ali.

17 One of the more noteworthy cases involved a freelance journalist named Taoufik Ben Brik who had established a reputation as one of the government's most vocal critics. In early 2000, Ben Brik waged a 43-day hunger strike to protest a travel ban that prevented him from leaving the country and other charges leveled against him because of articles he wrote for the European press on the human rights situation in Tunisia. The government relented and issued Ben Brik a new passport. Shortly after the end of the hunger strike, another journalist, Riad Ben

Fadhel, was seriously wounded in a drive-by shooting at his home near the presidential palace. Ben Fadhel had published an article in *Le Monde* that criticized the government's handling of the Ben Brik affair.

18 In November 2008, for example, Ben Ali ordered the release of the last twenty-one members of Ennahdha who had been jailed in the early 1990s. One of these prisoners, Sadok Chourou, was arrested again on December 3 for comments that he made in interviews with two media outlets about his time in prison and about contemporary politics in Tunisia. On December 13, a court in Tunis ruled that Chourou's comments, which included a call for the government to lift its ban on Ennahdha, violated Tunisia's law of associations. See Human Rights Watch (2009).

19 Interview with author in Tunis, June 9, 1993.

3 Stability, reform, and development in Tunisia's economy

1 Analysts use the term "rentier state" to describe economic and political systems that depend heavily on income from the sale of natural resources like oil and gas. Easy access to substantial income from these exports often hinders the growth of non-oil sectors (a phenomenon known as Dutch Disease), leaves the country's economy exposed to fluctuations in global oil and gas prices, reduces incentives for innovation, and fosters broad public reliance on the state for income and a wide range of goods and services. Politically, rentier economies allow rulers to use oil and gas receipts to buy public support and undermine demands for political representation. For more detailed discussions of rentier states, see Luciani (1990), Beblawi (1990).

2 For example, in 1953, Tunisia imported 1,000 tractors. In 1958, only 300 tractors came into the country (Toumi 1989: 54).

3 Concerns about a shortage of highly skilled labor may also have played a role in Bourguiba's decision to give the state a stronger role in economic planning. Between 1956 and 1963, Tunisia's French and Italian population dropped from about 150,000 to about 50,000 (Allman 1979: 51). While not all of these European workers were highly skilled or educated, and while their departure opened new opportunities for Tunisians, the exodus of Europeans did deprive Tunisia of considerable talent.

4 For a discussion of ISI and its application in the Arab world, see Richards and Waterbury (1990).

5 Algeria is the clearest example of a country that used hydrocarbon revenues to fund an ambitious industrialization effort. For overviews of Algeria's industrialization strategy, see Bennoune (1988), Tlemçani (1986), Al Kenz (1987, 1989).

6 In an effort to absorb rural unemployment, many coops employed three to four times as many workers as they needed (Allman 1979: 54).

7 For an overview of *infitah* across the Arab world, see Richards and Waterbury (1990: 238–62).

8 Heavy dependence on European economic conditions was one of the negative consequences of Tunisia's manufacturing growth in the 1970s. By 1976, 74 percent of Tunisia's manufacturing exports went to Europe. Over 50 percent of all manufacturing investment and nearly 90 percent of all new jobs were concentrated in sectors that depended heavily on exports to Europe (textiles, clothing, and leather goods). Thus, Europe's recession in the late 1970s had disastrous effects for Tunisia's manufacturing sector. Findlay (1984: 229) also notes that Tunisia's industrial growth in the 1970s was highly imbalanced in terms of sectors and regions. Some sectors received too much investment while other sectors remained neglected. Fifty-five percent of the new industrial firms created in

Tunisia in 1973–75 made their homes in Tunis or its immediate environs. This concentration created serious regional disparities across the country.

9 For more detailed discussions of the early phase of Tunisia's privatization program, see Harik (1992), Grissa (1991).

10 For overviews of Tunisia's economic relations with Europe, see White (2001) and Chneguir (2004).

11 Agricultural products continue to be a source of contention in trade talks between the EU and the Maghreb governments. Tunisian and EU authorities are currently preparing to negotiate an expansion of the free trade agreement that would take in the agriculture and service sectors (OECD 2008: 592).

12 For an overview of the *mise à niveau* program, see Murphy (2006).

13 US firms currently hold a 38 percent share of Tunisia's hydrocarbon exploration and production market. Because of its limited refining capacity, Tunisia's petroleum resources cover only 46 percent of its consumption needs. Tunisia's public enterprise for petroleum activities, ETAP, plans to drill approximately 75 new wells and to issue 44 new exploration permits between 2007–11. By 2010, government plans to have completed a new refinery in the Gulf of Gabes with a thirty-year concession to Qatar Petroleum International (OECD 2008: 589).

5 Stability, reform, and Tunisia's future

1 This oft-repeated quote has been reprinted several times over, including *The New York Times'* announcement of Bourguiba's death. See Pace (2000).

2 Quoted in Post and Robbins (1995: 163).

3 Quoted in Post and Robbins (1995: 163).

4 For more discussion of reform as an authoritarian "survival strategy" in the Arab world, see Ibrahim (1993).

5 It is worth noting that Francis Fukuyama's "end of history" thesis first appeared in *The National Interest* in 1989—the year when many began to realize that Ben Ali was not going to be democracy's architect in Tunisia. See Fukuyama (1989).

6 The literature on democratic transitions is vast. For useful theoretical starting points, see O'Donnell and Schmitter (1986); Przeworski (1991, 1995); Haggard and Kaufman (1995) and Casper and Taylor (1996). For a discussion with particular relevance to Tunisia, see Bellin (2002).

7 One of the most frequently-cited examples of this tension involves the controversy that erupted after a speech that Bourguiba gave on national television during Ramadan in 1964—the same year the Neo-Destour changed its name to the Destourian Socialist Party. During the month in which Muslims are forbidden to eat or drink from sunup to sundown, Bourguiba called for restaurants to remain open and proclaimed that a modern nation cannot afford to stop for a month every year. To dramatize his point, he made a point of drinking a glass of orange juice during his speech.

Bibliography

Abrouq, Nidal (2008) "Tunisian Products to Enjoy Duty-Free Status in US". Online. Available at: www.magharebia.com/cocoon/awi/xhtml1/en_GB/features/awi/features/2008/03/16/feature-02 (accessed 17 June 2009).

Abu Odeh, Adnan (2004) "The Collapse of the Tunis Summit". Online. Available at: www.carnegieendowment.org/arb/?fa = show&article = 21294 (accessed 20 June, 2009).

Abun Nasr, Jamil (1987) *A History of the Maghrib in the Islamic Period*, Cambridge: Cambridge University Press.

Achour, Habib (1989) *Enthousiasme et déceptions: ma vie politique et syndicale, 1944–1981*, Tunis: Alif.

African Development Bank (2006) "Tunisia: Country Strategy Paper, 2002–2004, 2006 Update". Online. Available at: http://www.afdb.org/en/documents/project-operations/country-strategy-papers/ (accessed 2 June 2006).

Al Fassi, Allal (1954) *The Independence Movements of Arab North Africa*, Washington, DC: American Council of Learned Societies.

Al Kenz, Ali (1987) *Le complexe sidérurgique d'el Hadjar: une expérience industrielle en Algérie*, Paris: CNRS.

—— (1989) *L'Algérie et la modernité*, Dakar: Conseil pour le Développement de la Recherche Économique et Sociale en Afrique.

Allman, James (1979) *Social Mobility, Education and Development in Tunisia*, Leiden: Brill.

Anderson, Lisa (1986) *The State and Social Transformation in Tunisia and Libya, 1830–1980*, Princeton, NJ: Princeton University Press.

—— (1987) "The State in the Middle East and North Africa", *Comparative Politics*, October, 1–18.

—— (1991) "Political Pacts, Liberalism and Democracy: The Tunisian National Pact of 1988", *Government and Opposition*, 26(2): 244–60.

Azaiez, Boubaker (1980) *Tels syndicalistes, tels syndicats*, Tunis: Éditions Imprimerie Tunis-Carthage.

—— (1983) *Le syndicalisme au possessif*, Sousse, Tunisia: Éditions Imprimerie Saidane.

Beau, Nicolas and Tuquoi, Jean-Pierre (1999) *Nôtre Ami Ben Ali: L'envers du "miracle tunisien"*, Paris: Éditions La Découverte.

Beblawi, Hazem (1990) "The Rentier State in the Arab World", in Giacomo Luciani (ed.) *The Arab State*, Berkeley, CA: University of California Press.

Belhassen, Souhayr (1988) "L'opposition introuvable", *Jeune Afrique*, 1454: 66.
Belkhodja, Tahar (1998) *Les trois décennies Bourguiba*, Paris: Éditions Arcanteres.
Bellin, Eva (1991) "Tunisian Industrialists and the State", in I. William Zartman (ed.) *Tunisia: The Political Economy of Reform*, Boulder, CO: Lynn Reinner.
—— (2002) *Stalled Democracy: Capital, Labor, and the Paradox of State-Sponsored Development*, Ithaca, NY: Cornell University Press.
Ben Dhiaf (1982) "Chronique politique tunisie", *Annuaire de l'Afrique du Nord 1982*, Paris: CNRS.
Ben Hamida (1989) *Le syndicalisme tunisien de la deuxième guerre mondiale à l'autonomie interne*, Tunis: Université de Tunis.
Ben Jelili, Riadh (2005) *Competition, Efficiency, and Competition Policy in Tunisia*. Online. Available at: www.idl-bnc.idrc.ca/dspace/bitstream/123456789/33289/1/28571.pdf (accessed 5 July 2009).
Ben Mansour, Khaled (1993) "Chedly Ayari et les années 70", *Réalités*, 386: 15–17.
Bennoune, Mahfoud (1988) *The Making of Contemporary Algeria, 1830–1987: Colonial Upheaval and Post-Independence Development*, Cambridge: Cambridge University Press.
Ben Romdhane, Mahmoud (1985) "Mutations économiques et socials et mouvement ouvrier en Tunisie de 1956 à 1980", in Nourredine Sraieb (ed.) *Le mouvement ouvrier maghrébin*, Paris: CNRS.
—— (1990) "Fondements et contenu des restructurations face à la crise économique en Tunisie", in Jean-Claude Santucci and Habib El Melki (eds.) *État et développement dans le monde arabe*, Paris: CNRS.
Burgat, Francois and Dowell, William (1993) *The Islamic Movement in North Africa*, Austin, TX: University of Texas Press.
Casper, Gretchen and Taylor, Michelle M. (1996) *Negotiating Democracy: Transitions from Authoritarian Rule*, Pittsburgh, PA: University of Pittsburgh Press.
Chneguir, Abdelaziz (2004) *La politique extérieure de la Tunisie 1957–1987*, Paris: L'Harmattan.
Coustillière, Jean-François (2005) "Méditerranée: 5+5 et initiative de sécurité", *Défense nationale*, 61(5): 76–82.
Dahmani, Abdelaziz (1989) "Tunisie: le 'non, mais . . .' de Ben Ali aux islamistes", *Jeune Afrique* 1485: 14–15.
Daoud, Zakya (1990) "Chronique Tunisienne", *Annuaire de l'Afrique du Nord 1989*, Paris: CNRS.
—— (1991) "Chronique Tunisienne", *Annuaire de l'Afrique du Nord 1990*, Paris: CNRS.
Dillman, Bradford (1998) "The Political Economy of Structural Adjustment in Tunisia and Algeria", *The Journal of North African Studies* 3(3): 1–24.
Dunn, Michael Collins (1994a) "The *Al-Nahda* Movement in Tunisia: From Renaissance to Revolution", in John Ruedy (ed.) *Islamism and Secularism in North Africa*, New York: St. Martin's Press.
—— (1994b) "Tunisia's New Elections Law Guaranteed Opposition a Voice". Online. Available at: www.washington-report.org/backissues/0494/9404020.htm (accessed 9 July, 2009).
Findlay, Allan M. (1984) "Tunisia: The Vicissitudes of Economic Development", in Richard I. Lawless and Allan M. Findlay (eds.) *North Africa: Contemporary Politics and Economic Development*, New York: St. Martin's Press.

Friends of Tunisia (2006) *Friends of Tunisia Newsletter* (March). Online. Available at: www.friendsofmorocco.org/FOTNews/March2006FOTnews.html (accessed 4 July, 2009).

Fukuyama, Francis (1989) "The End of History"? *The National Interest*, Summer.

Ghorbal, Samy (2003) "Notre ami Jacques Chirac", *Jeune Afrique*, 2238: 86–90.

—— (2009) "Comment l'UMA ne fonctionne pas". Online. Available at: www.jeuneafrique.com/Article/ARTJAJA2511p042–44.xml0/-anniversaire-commerce-UMA-Habib-Ben-Yahia-Comment-l-UMA-ne-fonctionne-pas.html (accessed 9 May, 2009).

Grissa, Abdelsatar (1991) "The Tunisian State Enterprises and Privatization Policy", in I. William Zartman (ed.) *Tunisia: The Political Economy of Reform*, Boulder, CO: Westview Press.

Guitta, Olivier (2007) "Terror in the Maghreb", *Weekly Standard*. Online. Available at: www.weeklystandard.com/Content/Public/Articles/000/000/013/284norib.asp (accessed 13 March 2007).

Haggard, Stephan and Kaufman, Robert R. (1995) *The Political Economy of Democratic Transitions*, Princeton, NJ: Princeton University Press.

Hani, Tahar (2008a) "Sarkozy's Mediterranean Challenge". Online. Available at: www.france24.com/en/20080711 (accessed 29 July, 2008).

—— (2008b) "UFM: The Key Dates". Online. Available at: www.france24.com/en/20080711 (accessed 29 July, 2008).

Harik, Iliya (1992) "Privatization and Development in Tunisia", in Iliya Harik and Denis J. Sullivan (eds.) *Privatization and Liberalization in the Middle East*, Bloomington, IN: Indiana University Press.

Henry, Clement (2007) "Tunisia's 'Sweet Little' Regime", in Robert Rotberg (ed.) *Worst of the Worst: Dealing with Repressive and Rogue Nations*, Washington, DC: Brookings Institution Press.

Human Rights Watch (2009) "Tunisia: Revolving Door Shows Intolerance for Dissent". Online. Available at: www.hrw.org/en/news/2009/03/12/tunisia-revolving-door-shows-intolerance-dissent.

Ibrahim, Saad Eddin (1993) "Crisis, Elites and Democratization in the Arab World", *Middle East Journal*, 47(2): 292–305.

International Monetary Fund (2008a) "Tunisia—Preliminary Conclusions of the Staff Visit". Online. Available at: www.imf.org/external/np/ms/2008/011608.htm (accessed 20 May, 2009).

—— (2008b) "Tunisia: Concluding Statement of the Article IV Consultation Mission". Online. Available at: www.imf.org/external/np/ms/2008/070908.html (accessed 6 July 2009).

—— (2009) "Statement of the IMF Mission on the 2009 Article IV Consultation with Tunisia". Online. Available at: www.imf.org/external/np/sec/pr/2009/pr09239.htm#TopOfPage.

Joffe, George (1999) "The European Union and the Maghreb in the 1990s", in Yahia H. Zoubir (ed.) *North Africa in Transition: State, Society and Economic Transformation in the 1990s*, Gainesville, FL: University Press of Florida.

Kaplan, Robert D. (2001) "Le Kef, Tunisia: Roman Africa", *The Atlantic Monthly*. Online. Available at: www.theatlanticmonthly.com/doc/prem/200106/Kaplan (accessed 31 May 2006).

Kleve, Jacob G. and Stolper, Wolfgang F. (1974) *Changes in Income Distribution, 1961–1971*, New York: United Nations Development Project.

Kraiem, Mustapha (1976) *Nationalisme et syndicalisme en Tunisie: 1918–1929*, Tunis: Union Générale Tunisienne du Travail.

—— (1996) *Mouvement national et Front Populaire: La Tunisie des années trente*, Tunis: Institut Supérieur d'Histoire du Mouvement National.

Lahmar, Mouldi (1994) *Du mouton à l'olivier*, Tunis: Cérès Productions.

Limam, Zyad (1989) "Ben Ali: L'heure des choix", *Jeune Afrique*, 1506: 37–43.

—— (1990) "Le temps des incertitudes", *Jeune Afrique*, 1559: 10–11.

—— (1992) "L'opposition en mal de chef", *Jeune Afrique*, 1665: 39.

Ling, Dwight (1967) *Tunisia: From Protectorate to Independence*, Bloomington, IN: Indiana University Press.

Liska, George (1963) *The Greater Maghreb: From Independence to Unity?* Washington, DC: The Washington Center of Foreign Policy Research.

Luciani, Giacomo (1990) "Allocation vs. Production States: A Theoretical Framework", in Giacomo Luciani (ed.) *The Arab State*, Berkeley, CA: University of California Press.

Mahjoubi, Ali (2004) "Comment Bourguiba voyait la question palestinienne", *Jeune Afrique*, 2241–42: 78–80.

Manai, Ahmed (1995) *Supplice tunisien: le jardin secret du Général Ben Ali*, Paris: Éditions La Découverte.

Marouki, Manoubi (1990) "Les huit propositions de l'opposition", *Réalités*, 1560: 33.

Meric, Edouard (1973) "The Destourian Socialist Party and the National Organizations", in I. William Zartman (ed.) *Man, State and Society in the Contemporary Maghreb*, New York: Praeger Publishers.

Micaud, Charles, Brown, Carl and Moore, Clement Henry (1964) *Tunisia: The Politics of Modernization*, New York: Praeger.

Moore, Clement Henry (1965) *Tunisia Since Independence: The Dynamics of One-Party Government*, Berkeley, CA: University of California Press.

—— (1966) *Tunisia After Bourguiba: Liberation or Political Degeneration?*, Princeton, NJ: Princeton University Press.

—— (1970) *Politics in North Africa*, Boston: Little, Brown and Company.

—— (1991) "Tunisian Banking: Policies for Adjustment and the Adjustment of Politics", in I. William Zartman (ed.) *Tunisia: The Political Economy of Reform*, Boulder, CO: Lynn Reinner.

Mortimer, Robert A. (1999) "The Arab Maghreb Union: Myth and Reality", in Yahia H. Zoubir (ed.) *North Africa in Transition: State, Society and Economic Transformation in the 1990s*, Gainesville, FL: University Press of Florida.

Murphy, Emma C. (1999) *Economic and Political Change in Tunisia: From Bourguiba to Ben Ali*, Basingstoke: Palgrave Macmillan.

—— (2006) "The Tunisian 'mise à niveau' Program and the Political Economy of Reform", *New Political Economy* 11:4, 519–40.

Nellis, John (1983) "A Comparative Assessment of the Development Performances of Algeria and Tunisia", *Middle East Journal*, 37(3): 370–93.

Nsouli, Saleh M., Bisat, Amer and Kanaan, Oussama (1996) "The European Union's New Mediterranean Strategy", *Finance and Development*, September, 14–17.

O'Donnell, Guillermo and Schmitter, Phillipe C. (1986) *Transitions from Authoritarian Rule: Tentative Conclusions about Uncertain Democracies*, Baltimore, MD: The Johns Hopkins University Press.

OECD (2008) "African Economic Outlook: Tunisia". Online. Available at: www.oecd.org/dataoecd/12/23/4578385.pdf (accessed 20 June 2009).

Pace, Eric (2000) "Habib Bourguiba, Independence Champion and President of Tunisia, Dies at 96", *New York Times*, 7 April, 2000.

Pakenham, Thomas (1991) *The Scramble for Africa: The White Man's Conquest of the Dark Continent from 1876 to 1912*, New York: Random House.

Pangaea Partners (1997) "Tunisia—Enters a New Phase". Online. Available at: www.pangaeapartners.com/tunpriv.html (accessed 24 July, 2007).

Pfeifer, Karen (1996) "Between Rocks and Hard Choices: International Finance and Economic Adjustment in North Africa", in Dirk Vandewalle (ed.) *North Africa: Development and Reform in a Changing Global Economy*, New York: St. Martin's Press.

Poncet, Jean (1970) "L'Économie tunisienne depuis l'indépendance", *Annuaire de l'Afrique du Nord 1969*, Paris: CNRS.

Post, Jerrold M. and Robins, Robert S. (1995) *When Illness Strikes the Leader: The Dilemma of the Captive King*, New Haven, CT: Yale University Press.

Prime Ministry of the Republic of Tunisia (2009) "Privatization in Tunisia". Online. Available at: www.privatizatoin.gov.tn/www/en/doc.asp?mcat=1&mrub= 49&msrub=4&dev=true (accessed 9 July 2009).

Przeworski, Adam (1991) *Democracy and the Market*, Cambridge: Cambridge University Press.

—— (1995) *Sustainable Democracy*, Cambridge: Cambridge University Press.

Réalités (2009) "Les partis de l'opposition: continueront-ils à filer un mauvais coton?". 16 March. Online. Available at: www.41.226.15.27/realites/home/ Realites-Lire-Article?=&a=1100300&t=161.

Republic of Tunisia (2005) "British Gas". Online. Available at: www.investintunisia. tn/site/en/article.php?id_article=649 (accessed 6 July 2009).

—— (2009) "Attractiveness for FDI". Online. Available at: www.investintunisia. tn/ site/en/article.php?id_article=836 (accessed 6 July 2009).

Richards, Alan and Waterbury, John (1990) *A Political Economy of the Middle East: State, Class and Economic Development*, Boulder, CO: Westview Press.

Rudebeck, Lars (1969) *Party and People: A Study of Political Change in Tunisia*, New York: Praeger.

Saghir, Jamal (1993) *Privatization in Tunisia*, Washington, DC: The World Bank.

Salem, Norma (1984) *Habib Bourguiba, Islam, and the Creation of Tunisia*, London: Croom Helm.

Seddon, David (1984) "Winter of Discontent: Economic Crisis in Tunisia and Morocco", *Merip Reports*, October: 7–19.

Sethom, Hafidh (1992) *Pouvior urbain et paysannerie en tunisie: qui seme le vent récolte la tempête*, Tunis: Cérès Productions.

Shahin, Emad Eldin (1997) *Political Ascent: Contemporary Islamic Movements in North Africa*, Boulder, CO: Westview Press.

Simons, Stefan (2008) "Nicolas Sarkozy's New 'Club Med.' ". Online. Available at: www.spiegel.de/international/europe0,1518,565667,00.html (accessed 29 July 2008).

Smith, Craig S. (2007) "Tunisia Is Feared to Be a New Base for Islamists", *International Herald Tribune*. Online. Available at: www.iht.com/articles/2007/02/20/ news/tunisia.php (accessed 13 March 2007).

Soudan, François and Belhassen, Souhayr (1989) "Élections tunisiennes: Ben Ali face aux Islamistes", *Jeune Afrique*, 1475: 13–15.

Soudan, François and Gharbi, Samir (1991) "Les islamistes, victimes de la guerre", *Jeune Afrique*, 1578: 50.

Stone, Russell A. (1982) "Tunisia: A Single Party System Holds Change in Abeyance", in I. William Zartman (ed.) *Political Elites in Arab North Africa*, New York: Longman.

Tlemçani, Rachid (1986) *State and Revolution in Algeria*, Boulder, CO: Westview Press.

Toumi, Mohsen (1989) *La tunisie de Bourguiba à Ben Ali*, Paris: Presses Universitaires de France.

Union Générale Tunisienne de Travail (1977) *Développement plus rapide, distribution plus equitable*, Tunis: Imprimerie de l'UGTT.

United States Department of State (2006) "Tunisia: Country Reports on Human Rights Practices-2005". Online. Available at: www.state.gov/g/drl/hrrpt/2005/61700. html (accessed 19 May 2006).

Vandewalle, Dirk (1988) "From the New State to the New Era: Toward a Second Republic in Tunisia", *Middle East Journal*, 42(4): 602–20.

—— (1992) "Ben Ali's New Era: Pluralism and Economic Privatization in Tunisia", in Henri J. Barkey (ed.) *The Politics of Economic Reform in the Middle East*, New York: St. Martin's Press.

—— (2006) *A History of Modern Libya*, Cambridge: Cambridge University Press.

Vivian, Herbert (1899) *Tunisia and the Modern Barbary Pirates*, New York: Longmans, Green and Company.

Volman, Daniel (1999) "Foreign Arms Sales and the Military Balance in the Maghreb", in Yahia H. Zoubir (ed.) *North Africa in Transition: State, Society and Economic Transformation in the 1990s*, Gainesville, FL: University Press of Florida.

Waltz, Susan (1986) "Islamist Appeal in Tunisia", *Middle East Journal*, 40(4): 651–70.

—— (1995) *Human Rights and Reform: Changing the Face of North African Politics*, Berkeley, CA: University of California Press.

Washington Times (2000) "International Special Report: Tunisia", July 10–14, 2000.

White, Gregory (2001) *A Comparative Economy of Tunisia and Morocco*, Albany, NY: State University of New York.

Wood, Pia Cristina (2002) "French Foreign Policy and Tunisia: Do Human Rights Matter"? *Middle East Policy*, IX(2): 92–110.

World Bank (2000) *Republic of Tunisia: Social and Structural Review 2000*, Washington, DC: The World Bank.

—— (2008) "New World Bank Study on Tunisia's Global Integration". Online. Available at: web.worldbank.org/WBSITE/EXTENAL/COUNTRIES/MENAEXT/TUNISIAEXTN/0,contentMDK:21945286~menuPK:310020~pagePK:2865066~piPK:2865079~theSitePK:310015,00.html. (accessed 5 July 2009).

World Economic Forum (2009) "The Africa Competitiveness Report 2009". Online. Available at: www.webforum.org/en/initiatites/gc/Africa%20Competitiveness%20Report/index.html (accessed 5 July 2009).

Zahar, Taieb (2008) "Et le rêve deviant réalité". Online. Available at: www.réalités.com.tn/home/ (accessed 25 July, 2008).

Zartman, I. William (1988) "Opposition as Support of the State", in Adeed Dawisha and I. William Zartman (eds.) *Beyond Coercion: The Durability of the Arab State*, Beckenham: Croom Helm.

—— (1991) "The Conduct of Political Reform: The Path Toward Democracy", in I. William Zartman (ed.) *Tunisia: The Political Economy of Reform*, Boulder, CO: Lynn Reinner.

Zghal, Abdelkader (1984) "La Tunisie: dernière république civile", *Jeune Afrique*, 1205: 34.

Zouari, Abderrazak (1990) "Aspects institutionnels du fonctionnement des marchés du travail", in Institut de financement du développement du maghreb arabe (ed.) *Politique de l'emploi en tunisie*. Tunis: Imprimeries Réunies.

Zouari, Jawed (1993) "Challenges to Tunisia's Privatization Policies", paper delivered at the annual meeting of the Middle East Studies Association of North America, 22–24 November.

Zoubir, Yahia H. and Zunes, Stephen (1999) "United States Policy in the Maghreb", in Yahia H. Zoubir (ed.) *North Africa in Transition: State, Society and Economic Transformation in the 1990s*, Gainesville, FL: University Press of Florida.

Index